Anonymous

Missionary Services and Hymnal

A manual for the use of Woman's and Young People's Missionary societies

Anonymous

Missionary Services and Hymnal
A manual for the use of Woman's and Young People's Missionary societies

ISBN/EAN: 9783337083953

Printed in Europe, USA, Canada, Australia, Japan

Cover: Foto ©Thomas Meinert / pixelio.de

More available books at **www.hansebooks.com**

Missionary Services

and

Hymnal.

A MANUAL

FOR THE USE OF

Woman's and Young People's

Missionary Societies.

"I will pray with the spirit and I will pray with the understanding also; I will sing with the spirit and I will sing with
the understanding also.—*I. Cor.* xiv. 15.

Price 35 Cents, Postage Paid.

Pu lish d by th: General Literature Committee of the Woman's
Home and Foreign Missionary Society of the
Lutheran Church (General Synod.)

2319 MARYLAND AVE., BALTIMORE, MD.

1895.

FIFTH EDITION WITH REVISION.

INTRODUCTION.

————✠————

An introduction to our MISSIONARY SERVICES AND HYMNAL need scarcely be given, though it has grown, and comes with a new name with this its fifth appearance, for the character remains unchanged.

It is still the helper, with sweet songs of loving service, precious promises from the Father to the children, and earnest petitions from the children to the Father: the latter to be used only when the full heart of the loving worshiper has not yet learned, unaided, to speak aloud its earnest desires.

Its mission is to "help those women who are gathered together, 'in His Name,' to say to all nations: 'Behold! the Lamb of God, which taketh away the sins of the world.'"

SUGGESTIONS.

To Leaders of Missionary Societies.

————✠————

1.   Prepare your programs carefully.   Avoid sameness.

2.   Select the hymns in advance, and notify those who will be asked to lead in prayer.

3.   Go to each meeting from your closet.

4.   Begin promptly.   Close at the appointed hour.

5.   The three great objects of your meeting are: (1) Prayer, (2) Study of the Word of God, (3) Dissemination of missionary intelligence.

6.   Subjects for Bible Lessons and Prayers, contained in the *Journal*, should be used.

7.   Many will offer a single petition in a circle of prayer, who would refuse to pray more at length.

8.   Keep your eyes open to fresh news of Christ's kingdom.

9.   Encourage regular and systematic giving.

10.   Make the exercises pointed and sprightly.

11.   Never be discouraged, even if the attendance is small, for the Master has said: "Where two or three are gathered together in my name, there will I be in the midst of them."

RULES OF ORDER.

The President shall rise and say:

1. The meeting will please come to order.

2. We will open our meeting with singing (prayer or scripture.)

3. The Recording Secretary will please call the roll.

4. The Recording Secretary will please read the minutes of the last meeting.

5. Are there any corrections?

6. If there are no corrections, the minutes stand approved as read.

7. Will the Corresponding Secretary please give her report?

8. What shall be done with this report?

   (*a*) A member, after rising, shall say: "Mrs. President, I move that the report be accepted."

   (*b*) Another member, after rising and addressing the President, shall say: "I second the motion."

9. It has been moved and seconded that the report be accepted. Are there any remarks?

10. All those favoring the motion will please say aye.

11. Those opposed, no.

12. The report is accepted. (Observe the same form with all the reports.)

13. We will now listen to the Treasurer's report.

14. Are there any reports from standing committees?

15. Are there any reports from special committees?

16. Is there any unfinished business?

17. Is there any new business?

18. We will now proceed to our program. (Program is here followed.)

19. A motion to adjourn is now in order. (Motion made as in 8-a-b.)

20. The meeting is adjourned.

GENERAL RULES.

1. All business shall be brought before the society in the form of a motion, as: "Mrs. President, I move that we send a box to our missionary."

2. Any member, in making a motion or any remarks, shall first rise and say: "Mrs. President." The President shall in turn recognize the member, calling her by name. After this the member may proceed to speak.

3. No remarks should be made upon a motion until it has been seconded.—*From Best Ideas.*

ORDER OF SERVICE, No. 1.

Consecration.

✠

RESPONSIVE READING.

Leader. *Present your bodies a living sacrifice, holy, acceptable unto God, which is your reasonable service.*

Response. Know ye not that your body is the temple of the Holy Ghost, which is in you, which ye have of God, and ye are not your own? for ye are bought with a price; therefore, glorify God in your body, and in your spirit, which are God's.

L. *They which live should not henceforth live unto themselves, but unto Him who died and rose again.*

R. And herein do I exercise myself, to have always a conscience void of offence toward God, and toward men.

L. *If any man be in Christ, he is a new creature; old things are passed away; behold all things are become new.*

R. The life which I now live in the flesh, I live by the faith of the Son of God, who loved me, and gave Himself for me.

L. *Whether therefore ye eat or drink, or whatsoever ye do, do all to the glory of God.*

R. For whether we live, we live unto the Lord: and whether we die, we die unto the Lord: Whether we live therefore, or die, we are the Lord's.

L. *Be ye steadfast, immovable, always abounding in the work of the Lord, forasmuch as ye know that your labor is not in vain in the Lord.*

R. Praying always with all prayer and supplication in the Spirit, and watching thereunto with all perseverance and supplication for all saints.

L. *Put on the whole armor of God, that ye may be able to stand against the wiles of the devil.*

R. For whosoever will save his life shall lose it; but whosoever shall lose his life for my sake and the Gospel's, the same shall save it.

L. *What doth the Lord require of thee?*

R. To do justly, and love mercy, and walk humbly with thy God.

L. *Who then is willing to consecrate his service this day unto the Lord?*

R. Behold we come unto thee; for thou art the Lord our God. We will serve the Lord.

L. *Consecrate yourselves to-day to the Lord, that he may bestow upon you a blessing:*

All. Behold, I come quickly; and my reward is with me, to give every man according as his work shall be.

PRAYER.

Dear Father, we come into Thy presence rejoicing that Thou art the bountiful Giver of all good gifts. We know that when Thou didst give us Thine only beloved Son, that with Him Thou art ready "freely to give us all things." We want now the outpouring of Thy holy Spirit, to fit us for the consecrated service Thou dost require, and which we are desirous of rendering to Thee. Show us how to place ourselves in Thy hands, as clay in the hands of the potter, rejoicing to be moulded even into the homely earthen vessel, if only we are able to carry the precious water of life, to revive the thirsty souls of Thy children who are perishing in the desert of this weary, sin-stricken world.

We beseech Thee, open our eyes to see all the riches of glory in Christ Jesus, and to know the joy of a full surrender of all we are and have, to *His* service, in serving and rescuing Thy lost sheep all over the world. Warm our hearts with the tender, compassionate, self-sacrificing love Thou didst manifest to those who were wandering in the wilderness of sin. May the sad, Christless condition of our brothers and sisters, everywhere, be borne in upon our spirits, until we are ready to sacrifice to enable them to hear the glad tidings. May we ever bear their sorrows on our hearts when we come before the mercy seat.

We know it is Thy will that *all* should come to the knowledge of the truth: may we have grace to labor zealously for the accomplishment of that will. We know it is our privilege, by prevailing prayer, to call down blessings on our beloved workers, and to strengthen their hands; so we beseech Thee to send down showers of blessings on every laborer in Thy vineyard; uphold, strengthen, and reward each one with an abundant harvest, and may we share with them, the joy of bringing in the sheaves to lay at Thy feet on the last great day.

We ask all in the name of our dear Redeemer. Amen.

ORDER OF SERVICE, No. 2.

Christ's Kingdom.

✠

RESPONSIVE READING.

Leader. *The kings of the earth set themselves, and the rulers take counsel together, against the Lord, and against his Anointed.*

Response. Yet have I set my King upon my holy hill of Zion.

L. *Lift up your heads, O ye gates; and be ye lifted up, ye everlasting doors; and the King of glory shall come in.*

R. Who is this King of glory?

L. *The Lord strong, and mighty, the Lord mighty in battle:*

R. The Lord of hosts, he is the King of glory.

L. *Rejoice greatly, O daughter of Zion; shout O daughter of Jerusalem: behold, thy King cometh unto thee;*

R. And his dominion shall be from sea even to sea, and from the river unto the ends of the earth.

L. *Him hath God exalted with His right hand to be a Prince, and a Saviour.*

R. To Him be glory and dominion, forever and ever.

L. *Jesus answered. My kingdom is not of this world: if My kingdom were of this world, then would My servants fight.*

R. For the kingdom of God is not meat, and drink, but righteousness, and peace, and joy in the Holy Ghost.

L. *I will declare the decree: the Lord hath said unto me, Thou art my Son; this day have I begotten thee.*

R. Ask of me, and I shall give thee the heathen for thine inheritance, and the uttermost parts of the earth for thy possession.

L. *They that dwell in the wilderness shall bow before him; and his enemies shall lick the dust.*

R. Yea, all kings shall fall down before him; all nations shall serve him.

L. *Of the increase of his government and peace there shall be no end.*

R. And the Lord shall be King over all the earth: in that day shall there be one Lord, and his name one.

L. *And there were great voices in heaven, saying, The kingdoms of this world are become the kingdoms of our Lord, and of his Christ.*

R. And he shall reign forever, and ever.

PRAYER.

Let "Thy kingdom come, oh our Father, and
Thy will be done on earth as it is in heaven."
We have come to do Thy will, and we have
come with the earnest desire to extend Thy
kingdom. Thou dost bid us "go and make disciples of all nations," and with the command,
Thou hast given Thy word that the day shall
come "when every knee shall bow, and every
tongue confess, that Thou art Lord, to the glory
of God the Father." Dear Jesus, we beseech of
Thee, hasten that day; we long to see the whole
earth own Thee King. Thou knowest we some-
times are discouraged because the time seems so
long, and we accomplish so little, and yet Thou
hast said Thou wouldst bring it to pass. The
work is Thine, Thou great Master-Builder; we
are only co-workers with Thee. Forbid that we
should think, because we can do but little, Thou
hast no need of us, and so fold our one talent
in a napkin. We know Thou hast as much need
of the one as of the ten; then help us to consecrate all, be it one or ten, to Thee.

Bless our meeting together; may we realize it
has not been in vain: send us to our homes
strengthened in faith, and with a determined
purpose to labor more faithfully for Thee. We
would not forget to pray for our missionaries,
who have gone in our place. They have made
it possible for us to obey Thee in Thy last command, and yet stay in our homes, because, while

we may not literally go, we can help to send.
Oh, do Thou bless them; give them strength for
their weakness: give them a double portion of
Thy love, and prosper them in all they undertake in Thy Name. And we pray, dear Lord,
for the women of our churches who are indiffer-
ent to this great work. Make them feel their
responsibility, and may they not rest satisfied
with their own salvation, but may they be willing to help save others. And now, our Father,
forgive our many sins, give us pure hearts and
earnest purposes, and when Thou art done with
our laboring and serving here below, grant us
an abundant entrance into Thy kingdom, for
Jesus' sake. Amen.

ORDER OF SERVICE, No. 3.

Christ Victorious.

✠

RESPONSIVE READING.

Leader. *And it shall come to pass, in the last days, that the mountain of the Lord's house shall be established in the top of the mountains, and shall be exalted above the hills; and all nations shall flow into it.*

Response. And I will make all my mountains a way, and my highways shall be exalted.

Behold these shall come from far; and lo, these from the north and from the west; and these from the land of Sinim.

L. *And I, if I be lifted up from the earth, will draw all men unto me.*

R. Lift up thine eyes round about, and behold; all these gather themselves together, and come to thee.

L. *And if any man sin, we have an advocate with the Father, Jesus Christ the righteous.*

R. And he is the propitiation for our sins; and not for our sins only, but also for the sins of the whole world.

L. *And they sang a new song, saying, Thou art worthy to take the book, and to open the seals thereof; for thou wast slain, and hast redeemed us to God by thy blood, out of every kindred, and tongue, and people, and nation.*

R. After this I beheld, and lo, a great multitude, which no man could number, of all nations, and kindreds, and people, and tongues, stood before the throne, and before the Lamb, clothed with white robes, and palms in their hands.

L. *And cried with a loud voice, saying, Salvation to our God, which sitteth upon the throne, and unto the Lamb.*

R. For whosoever shall call upon the name of the Lord, shall be saved.

L. *How then shall they call upon him in whom they have not believed? And how shall they believe on him of whom they have not heard? And how shall they hear without a preacher?*

R. Go ye, therefore, and teach all nations, baptizing them in the name of the Father, and of the Son, and of the Holy Ghost.

PRAYER.

Thou seest, dear Lord, before Thee, a little band of Thy soldiers and servants, who are ready and desirous to march and to serve. But, in order to do so, we feel the necessity of being equipped for the battle with the whole "armor of God." We know the sword of the Spirit is invincible, but how shall we wield it? We know "the word of God is quick and powerful—sharper than any two-edged sword." But how shall we utter it? We beseech Thee to be our drill-master, and train us to fight the good fight of faith, that we may do our part to conquer the world for Christ.

At the word of command—"Go"—may we be enabled to start forward and keep step with that great company, who have ever pressed to the front, to storm the forts of heathendom, counting not their lives dear, but gladly laying all at the foot of the Cross.

We know this warfare is the serious business of our lives, and we pray Thee, keep us from the entanglements of worldliness and vanity, and from being too much absorbed with the cares of this life. We are so prone to stray out of the ranks, and lag behind. May it be our ambition to keep in the forefront of the battle, to be ever on the alert, with our weapons in our hands; may we be strong and courageous in the strength of our God, to fight evil and put to rout all the hosts of Satan.

We know that, in order to be victorious, we must keep very close to our great Captain, be very attentive to His orders, obey promptly and to the letter. Give us grace to do so, that we may have our part in the last great victory over all the powers of evil, and be enabled to

shout "Allelujah! for the Lord God Omnipotent reigneth." "The kingdoms of this world
have become the kingdoms of our God, and of
his Christ."

We ask all in the name of our adorable Redeemer, and we know it is according to His will,
and we claim the promise, if we ask anything
according to His will, He heareth it. Amen.

ORDER OF SERVICE, No. 4.

The Almighty Redeemer.

✠

RESPONSIVE READING.

(*All standing.*)

Leader. *Look unto me, and be ye saved, all the ends of the earth; for I am God, and there is none else.*

Response. But thou, O Lord, art a God full of compassion, gracious, long-suffering, and plenteous in mercy and truth.

L. *The Lord hath made bare his holy arm in the eyes of all the nations; and all the ends of the earth shall see the salvation of our God.*

R. All nations whom thou hast made shall come and worship before thee, O Lord, and shall glorify thy name.

L. *Seek ye the Lord while he may be found: call ye upon him, while he is near.*

R. O thou that hearest prayer, unto thee shall all flesh come.

L. *Ho, every one that thirsteth, come ye to the waters, and he that hath no money, come ye, buy and eat; yea, come, buy wine and milk without money, and without price.*

R. For the promise is unto you, and to your children, and to all that are afar off, even as many as the Lord our God shall call.

L. *For God so loved the world, that he gave his only begotten Son, that whosoever believeth in him should not perish, but have everlasting life.*

R. And being found in fashion as a man, he humbled himself, and became obedient unto death, even the death of the cross.

L. *And that every tongue should confess that Jesus Christ is Lord, to the glory of God the Father.*

R. That at the name of Jesus every knee should bow, of things in heaven, and things in earth, and things under the earth.

L. *And ye will not come to me, that ye might have life.*

R. All that the Father giveth me shall come to me: and him that cometh to me, I will in no wise cast out.

L. *But whosoever drinketh of the water that I shall give him shall never thirst; but the water that I shall give him shall be in him a well of water, springing up into everlasting life.*

R. And the Spirit and the bride say, Come. And let him that heareth say, Come. And let him that is athirst come. And whosoever will, let him take the water of life freely.

CHANT.

Glory be to the Father, and to the Son, and to the Holy Ghost.

As it was in the beginning, is now, and ever shall be, world without end. Amen.

PRAYER.

O Lord, Thou art great; and doest wondrous things. Thou art God alone. Among the gods there is none like Thee, neither are there any works like unto Thy works. Thou doest all things according to Thy pleasure, and all that Thou doest is wise and good. Thy mercy is in the heavens, and Thy truth reacheth unto the clouds.

With unfeigned submission to Thy authority, and reverence for Thy majesty, and gratitude for Thy goodness, do we, Thy handmaidens, come before Thy throne of grace this hour.

To Thee, who art our merciful Father, and in Christ, our Almighty Redeemer, and in the Holy Ghost, our Comforter and Sanctifier, do we lift up our hearts, and offer unto Thee our worship.

We adore and give Thee thanks; for Thy mercy to us is very great, and endureth forever. We thank Thee for Thy Word, in which Thou dost reveal the great love wherewith Thou hast loved us, even when we were dead in trespasses and in sin, in sending Thy dear Son to suffer and die in our stead, that we might have redemption through His blood, and be made heirs of eternal life. Thanks be ever unto Thee for this unspeakable gift.

Gracious God, forgive all our sins, and let Thy presence and blessing abide with all assembled here, and let the words of our mouths and the meditations of our hearts be acceptable in Thy sight.

Lord, help us to do all we can to adorn the doctrine of our Saviour, to advance His cause, and to promote the honor of His name.

Knowing the preciousness of Thy forgiving love in our own experience, may we commend it to our fellow-men. May we contemplate the world of mankind with something of the love with which Jesus looked upon it, and grant us to feel somewhat of the compassion with which He yearned for its conversion.

As we seek to take an humble part in spreading the glad tidings of the Gospel, direct us in all our ways, to the end that Thy cause may be greatly prospered in our hands.

O Holy Spirit, be Thou our counselor, and let Thy abundant wisdom abide in all our hearts, that the plans and means we employ to save others may all be chosen and blessed of Thee.

Crown the labors of all our missionaries with great success, and may we who labor in the Gospel with them have the unspeakable joy of seeing the work of the Lord prosper in their hands.

And unto Him that loved us, and washed us from our sins in His own blood, be glory and dominion, forever and ever. Amen.

ORDER OF SERVICE, No. 5.

The Sure Foundation.

✠

RESPONSIVE READING.

Leader. *Therefore thus saith the Lord God, Behold, I lay in Zion for a foundation stone, a tried stone, a precious corner stone, a sure foundation: he that believeth shall not make haste.*

Response. For other foundation can no man lay than that is laid, which is Jesus Christ.

L. *Upon this rock I will build my church; and the gates of hell shall not prevail against it.*

R. Jesus saith unto them, Did ye never read in the Scriptures, The stone which the builders rejected, the same is become the head of the corner: this is the Lord's doing, and it is marvelous in our eyes.

L. *For we are laborers together with God: ye are God's husbandry ye are God's building.*

R. And are built upon the foundation of the apostles, and prophets, Jesus Christ himself being the chief cornerstone;

L. *In whom all the building, fitly framed together, groweth unto an holy temple in the Lord.*

R. In whom ye also are builded together for an habitation of God, through the Spirit.

L. *Therefore will we not fear, though the earth be removed, and the mountains be carried into the midst of the sea.*

R. The Lord of hosts is with us; the God of Jacob is our refuge.

L. *They that. trust in the Lord shall be as Mount Zion, which cannot be moved, but abideth forever.*

R. As the mountains are round about Jerusalem, so the Lord is round about his people from h nceforth, even forever.

L. *What shall we then say to these things? If the Lord be for us, who can be against us?*

R. He that spared not his own Son, but delivered him up for us all, how shall he not with him also freely give us all things?

L. *Who shall separate us from the love of Christ? Shall tribulation, or distress, or persecution, or famine, or nakedness, or peril, or the sword?*

R. Nay, in all these things, we are more than conquerors, through him that loved us.

PRAYER.

O God, Thou art the rock of our salvation. Before the mountains were brought forth, or ever Thou hadst formed the earth, even from everlasting to everlasting, Thou art God. We would come to Thee in confidence, our Father, feeling that, although the storms of life assail

us, and we are beset on the right and on the
left with difficulties, yet our hope may rest securely on Thee. Help us, day by day, to have
Christ so manifested in our lives that, though
Thy book of nature may be a closed book to
many, and Thy written Word a neglected Book,
yet may we be, indeed, living epistles or books,
known and read of all men. Our Father, may
we so labor together with Thee for the upbuilding and extension of Thy kingdom, realizing
that "other foundation can no man lay than
that is laid, which is Jesus Christ," and that
if our work be builded upon Him, it cannot fail,
but will abide, even as Thou, O God, dost
abide, unto all eternity. We beseech Thee that
Thou wilt give to every one in Thy presence according to their needs. Every good and every
perfect gift is from above, and cometh down
from the Father of lights, with whom is no var-
iableness, neither shadow of turning. There is.
none other to whom we can go. If we want wisdom or truth, they are Thy attributes, and out
of Thy fullness, Thou art so ready to grant even
more abundantly than we can ask. Grant us
Thy Holy Spirit, that even in our thoughts we
may keep close to Thee; and when we have done
Thy will upon earth, may we inherit that kingdom prepared for Thy people from the foundation of the world, and to Thy name shall be all
the glory forever. Amen.

ORDER OF SERVICE, No. 6.

Praise Service, No. 1.

✠

RESPONSIVE READING.

Leader. *Let the heavens be glad, and let the earth rejoice; and let men say among the nations, the Lord reigneth.*

Response. All the earth shall worship thee, and shall sing unto thee: they shall sing to thy name.

L. *Let the heavens and earth praise him, the seas, and everything that moveth therein.*

R. Oh, sing unto the Lord a new song: sing unto the Lord all the earth.

L. *For the Lord is great, and greatly to be praised: he is to be feared above all gods.*

R. All the kings of the earth shall praise him, O Lord, when they hear the words of thy mouth.

L. *It is a good thing to give thanks unto the Lord, and to sing praises unto thy name, O most High:*

R. To show forth thy loving kindness in the morning, and thy faithfulness every night.

L. *I will bless the Lord at all times: his praise shall continually be in my mouth.*

R. My soul shall make her boast in the Lord: the humble shall hear thereof, and be glad.

L. *O magnify the Lord with me, and let us exalt his name together.*

R. Thus will I bless thee while I live: I will lift up my hands in thy name.

L. *Enter into his gates with thanksgiving, and into his courts with praise:*

R. Open to me the gates of righteousness: I will go into them, and I will praise the Lord.

L. *So we, thy people, and sheep of thy pasture, will give thee thanks forever: we will show forth thy praise to all generations.*

R. One generation shall praise thy works to another, and shall declare thy mighty acts.

All. Blessed be the Lord God of Israel, from everlasting to everlasting, and let all the people say, Amen.

PRAYER.

Oh, God, our God, we thank thee that thou hast endowed thy sanctuary with beauty and grace; that in Zion thou dost appear, and that the glory of thy presence is manifest to every contrite heart. We thank thee, that thou hast chosen us to dwell in thy courts, for we shall be still praising thee. We praise thee, that thou art the confidence of all the earth; that thou hearest prayer, and unto thee shall all flesh come. We praise thee for thy power, which ruleth the world; that power which setteth the mountains, stilleth the noise of the seas, and the tumult of the people; that power which extendeth to the uttermost parts of the earth, and maketh the outgoings of the mornings and evenings to rejoice. We praise thee, that thou visitest the earth, and enrichest it with the river of God. We praise thee for the refreshing showers and the green pastures, which are clothed with flocks. And, above all, we praise thee for thy great salvation, and thy glory, which we declare among the heathen. But, while we praise thee, we also implore thee that, as thou hast sent refreshing showers upon the earth, and causeth it to spring forth in rich fruitage, thou wilt send showers of blessings into our hearts, that we may be renewed in spirit, strengthened in thy work, and enabled to bring forth fruit abundant unto thy harvest. We implore thy gracious presence to be with us always, for the sake of thy dear Son. Amen.

ORDER OF SERVICE, No. 7.

Praise Service, No. 2.

✠

RESPONSIVE READING.

Leader. *Sing, O daughter of Zion; shout, O Israel; be glad and rejoice with all thy heart, O daughter of Jerusalem.*

Response. I will praise thee, O Lord, with my whole heart; I will show forth all thy marvelous works.

L. *Sing praises to God, sing praises; sing praises unto our King, sing praises.*

R. Thou art my God, and I will praise thee; thou art my God, and I will exalt thee.

L. *Sing unto the Lord, bless his name: show forth his salvation from day to day.*

R. I will sing unto the Lord as long as I live; I will sing praise to my God while I have any being.

L. *Sing, O ye heavens, for the Lord hath done it; shout, ye lower parts of the earth; break forth into singing, ye mountains, O forests, and every tree therein; for the Lord hath redeemea Jacob, and glorified himself in Israel.*

R. All thy works shall praise thee, O Lord; and thy saints shall bless thee.

L. *And Mary said, my soul doth magnify the Lord.*

R. And my spirit hath rejoiced in God my Saviour.

L. *And suddenly there was with the angel a multitude of the heavenly host, praising God.*

R. Saying, Amen: Blessing, and glory, and wisdom, and thanksgiving, and honor and power and might, be unto our God for ever and ever.

L. *Sing unto him, sing psalms unto him.*

R. O Lord, open thou my lips, and my mouth shall shew forth thy praise.

L. *And in that day shall ye say, Praise the Lord, call upon his name, declare his doings among the people, make mention that his name is exalted.*

R. Bless the Lord, O my soul; and all that is within me, bless his holy name.

L. *And ye shall eat in plenty and be satisfied, and praise the name of the Lord your God, that hath dealt wondrously with you: and my people shall never be ashamed.*

R. Thou art my God, and I will praise thee: thou art my God, and I will exalt thee.

L. *Praise ye the Lord. Praise ye the name of the Lord; praise him, O ye servants of the Lord.*

R. Glory to God in the highest, **and on earth** peace, good-will toward men.

L. *Now unto him that is able to keep you from falling, and to present you faultless before the presence of his glory with exceeding joy,*

And from Jesus Christ, who is the faithful witness, and the first begotten of the dead, and the Prince of the kings of the earth; unto him that loved us, and washed us from our sins in his own blood; and hath made us kings and priests unto God and his Father; to him be glory and dominion forever and ever. Amen.

(Gospel Hymns, No. 25.)

We praise Thee, O God, for the Son of Thy love,
For Jesus, who died and is now gone above.

CHORUS.

Hallelujah! Thine the glory. Hallelujah, amen.
Hallelujah! Thine the glory. Revive us again.

We praise Thee, O God, for Thy Spirit of light,
Who has shown us our Saviour, and scattered our night.
—CHO.

All glory and praise to the God of all grace,
Who has bought us, and sought us, and guided our ways.
—CHO.

Revive us again; fill each heart with Thy love;
May each soul be rekindled with fire from above.—CHO.

PRAYER.

Our Father, who art in heaven, etc.

ORDER OF SERVICE, No. 8.

The Precious Saviour.

✠

To God, the Father, Son,
And Spirit, One in Three,
Be glory as it was, is now,
And shall forever be.

RESPONSIVE READING.

(*All standing.*)

Leader. *And I will set up one shepherd over them, and he shall feed them; he shall feed them, and he shall be their shepherd.*

Response. I am the good shepherd: the good shepherd giveth his life for the sheep.

L. *He is brought as a lamb to the slaughter, and as a sheep before her shearers is dumb, so he opened not his mouth.*

R. Behold the Lamb of God, which taketh away the sin of the world.

L. *He shall feed his flock like a shepherd; he shall gather the lambs with his arm, and carry them in his bosom.*

R. He will deliver them out of all places, where they have been scattered, in the cloudy and dark day.

L. *And this is his name, whereby he shall be called,* THE LORD OUR RIGHTEOUSNESS.

R. But of him are ye in Christ Jesus, who
of God is made unto us righteousness and sanct-
ification and redemption.

L. *Behold, I lay in Zion for a foundation
stone, a tried stone, a precious corner stone, a
sure foundation.*

R. Unto you, therefore, which believe, he is
precious; but unto them which be disobedient,
the stone which the builders disallowed, the
same is made the head of the corner.

L. *In that day there shall be a fountain opened
in the house of David for sin and for uncleanness.*

R. Forasmuch as ye know that ye were not
redeemed with corruptible things, but with the
precious blood of Christ, as a lamb without
blemish and without spot.

All. Unto him that loved us, and washed us
from our sins in his own blood, and hath made
us kings and priests unto God and his Father,
to him be glory and dominion forever and ever.

PRAYER.

O Thou who dwellest in the high and holy
place—but who condescendeth to dwell also with
the contrite and humble of spirit—we adore Thee
as our Creator and Preserver, our bountiful
Benefactor, and loving Friend. We rejoice
that we can look up to Thee, the mightiest of all
Beings, and call Thee by that dear name that
dispels all misgivings, "Our Father, who art in

heaven." The kindest of earthly parents could not so long have borne with our ingratitude and waywardness, but Thy compassions fail not; Thou rememberest that we are dust, and hast graciously declared, "I will be a Father unto you."

O, Jesus! Thou blessed Elder Brother! Thou Precious Saviour, of whom the whole family in heaven and earth is named, we implore Thee to shine in our hearts, with "the brightness of Thy rising." May we enjoy union and communion with Thee. May a sense of Thy favor pervade all our duties, sanctify our blessings, and lighten our trials. May the realized assurance that Thou art with us dispel every misgiving and dry every tear. May we hear Thee, even now, saying, "Lo, I am with you alway."

And we not only pray for Thy comforting presence in our hearts; we would pray for the extension of Thy kingdom throughout the world. "Arise, O God, and let Thine enemies be scattered." May the glorious time soon come when "habitations of darkness and horrid cruelty" shall no longer pollute the earth, when Jew and Gentile shall unite to welcome the Prince of Peace to the throne of universal empire, and all the ends of the earth shall see the salvation of our God. Come, Lord Jesus, come quickly.

And to Father, Son, and ever Blessed Spirit, shall be ascribed all praise, honor, and glory; world without end. Amen.

ORDER OF SERVICE, No. 9.

Witnessing.

✠

RESPONSIVE READING.

Leader. *Whosoever therefore shall confess me before men, him will I confess also before my Father which is in heaven.*

Response. We believe, and are sure, that thou art the Christ, the Son of the living God.

L. *Ye are my witnesses, saith the Lord, that I am God.*

R. To him give all the prophets witness, that, through his name, whosoever believeth in him shall receive remission of sins.

L. *A true witness delivereth souls; but a deceitful witness speaketh lies.*

R. Let your lightso shine before men, that they may see your good works, and glorify your Father, which is in heaven.

L. *This I say therefore, and testify in the Lord, that ye henceforth walk not as other Gentiles walk, in the vanity of their mind.*

R. The Spirit itself beareth witness with our spirit, that we are the children of God.

L. *Be ye therefore followers of God as dear children.*

R. He commanded us to preach unto the people, and to testify that it is he which was ordained of God to be the Judge of the quick and the dead.

L. *The things that thou hast heard of me among many witnesses, the same commit thou to faithful men who shall be able to teach others also.*

R. We preach not ourselves, but Christ Jesus, the Lord.

L. *Study to show thyself approved unto God, a workman that needeth not to be ashamed.*

R. Hereby know we that we dwell in him, and he is in us, because he hath given us of his Spirit, and we have seen, and do testify, that the Father sent the Son to be the Saviour of the world.

L. *He that saith he abideth in him ought also to walk, even as he walked.*

R. Therefore if any man be in Christ, he is a new creature.

L. *Forasmuch as ye are manifestly declared to be the epistle of Christ, written not with ink, but with the Spirit of the living God. Ye also shall bear witness.*

R. That at the name of Jesus every knee should bow, and that every tongue should confess that Jesus Christ is the Lord.

PRAYER.

Dear Heavenly Father, we would come very near unto Thee. We feel our unworthiness to come into Thy presence, and to be called Thy children, but we would come pleading the love of Him who gave Himself for us, even when we were far off from Thee. O we pray Thee, our Father, that Thy Holy Spirit may be poured out upon us, that we may be filled with the knowledge of Thy will in all wisdom and spiritual understanding; and may we walk worthy of the Lord, being fruitful in every good work, and increasing in the knowledge of God, that our lives may testify to the world that we have been with Christ, and learned of Him. More and more, may our life be hid in Thine, and may we have the witness of our conscience that, day by day, we are living nearer the Spirit, and example of our Master. As Thou didst come to earth and live not for self, but to save us, so may we seek to forget self, and live to witness for Thee, and for the sake of others. May many willing hearts be ready to testify of Thy truth to the nations that are yet in darkness, for we realize that Thy love is not bound; it is not for our nation, or people, but whosoever will, may come. Wilt Thou hasten the time when the kingdoms of the earth shall become the kingdoms of our Lord, and every creature shall know Thee, whom to know is life eternal; and to Thy honor and glory shall be praise evermore. Amen.

We thank Thee, blessed Master, Thyself the great Witness, that we may witness for Thee, and for the power of the Gospel, in a world needing nothing so much as the knowledge of Thy love. We bless Thee for every true, pure, unselfish, and loving life, for all whose light shines in the midst of darkness. So enlighten and renew us, by the power of Thy Word and Spirit, that each of us may be a living epistle of Christ, known and read of all men. We mourn and confess our frailties and sins, and lament that so often our living does not honor the Saviour, whose servants we are. There is forgiveness with Thee, O Thou who wast tempted in all points, like as we are. Help us to put from us the sins that so easily beset us, that we may shine as lights in the world, holding forth the word of life. So baptize us, and all Thy dear people, with the spirit of all grace and supplication, that the world may take knowledge of us, that we have been with Christ, and have learned of Him. In our homes make us patterns of piety, and whilst in the world, forbid that any of us should be of it; but may we walk worthy of our high calling, and adorn the doctrine of God, our Saviour, in all things. Save us from the love of money; and fill us with an all-consuming zeal for the coming of the kingdom of Christ. Bless our fellow-laborers, making them strong in the time of trial, faithful unto the end. We ask all in His name, whose servants we are, and to whom shall be the glory forever. Amen.

ORDER OF SERVICE, No. 10.

The Loving Call.

✠

Come ye that love the Lord,
And let your joys be known;
Join in a song of sweet accord,
Whilst we surround the throne.

RESPONSIVE READING.

(*All standing.*)

Leader. *Come ye, and let us go up to the mountain of the Lord, to the house of the God of Jacob, and he will teach us of his ways, and we will walk in his paths.*

Response. I was glad when they said unto me, Let us go unto the house of the Lord.

L. *O come, let us worship, and bow down; let us kneel before the Lord our Maker.*

R. When thou saidst, Seek ye my face, my heart said unto thee, thy face, Lord, will I seek.

L. *Come, and let us return unto the Lord; for he hath torn, and he will heal us; he hath smitten, and he will bind us up.*

R. Fear thou not, for I am with thee; be not dismayed, for I am thy God; I will strengthen thee; yea, I will help thee; yea, I will uphold thee with the right hand of my righteousness.

L. *Come thou with us, and we will do thee good.*

R. For whither thou goest, I will go; and where thou lodgest, I will lodge; thy people shall be my people, and thy God my God.

L. *Come thou and all thy house into the ark.*

R. But as for me and my house, we will serve the Lord.

L. *Ho. every one that thirsteth, come to the waters; and he that hath no money, come ye, buy and eat; yea, buy wine and milk, without money and without price.*

R. But whosoever drinketh of the water that I shall give him shall never thirst; but the water that I shall give him shall be in him a well of water springing up into everlasting life.

L. *Incline your ear and come unto me; hear, and your soul shall live; and I will make an everlasting covenant with you, even the sure mercies of David.*

R. Him that cometh to me, I will in no wise cast out.

L. *Come unto me, all ye that labor and are heavy-laden, and I will give you rest.*

R. Cast thy burden upon the Lord, and he shall sustain thee; he shall never suffer the righteous to be moved.

L. *And the Spirit and the bride say, Come. And let him that heareth say, Come. And let him* *that is athirst come. And whosoever will, let him take of the water of life freely.*

R. For I will pour water upon him that is thirsty, and floods upon the dry ground: I will pour my Spirit upon thy seed, and my blessing upon thy offspring.

L. *Come, ye blessed of my Father, inherit the kingdom prepared for you from the foundation of the world.*

R. He that overcometh shall inherit all things; and I will be his God, and he·shall be my son.

PRAYER.

Our Father, who art in heaven, we gladly respond to Thy loving call, and present ourselves before Thy throne. Our hearts hunger and yearn for Thy love. Thy word is so full of rich promises to those who hear and obey Thy voice, that we would willingly yield ourselves to Thee, and receive Thy sweet and precious blessings.

The Spirit and Bride have told us to come; Jesus Christ has told us how to come. We thank Thee that He is the Way, the Guide, and the Light. We thank Thee that He accompanies us, and leads us unto Thyself. Let no sin separate us from Thy side, O God. Keep back Thy servants from all presumptuous sins, and cleanse us thoroughly. We praise Thee that Thou hast not only called us out from among the sinners, but hast also commanded us to go and preach Thy loving Word to all nations. We are weak, and unworthy of this honor. As far as lieth in us, we pray that we may be used by Thee in the advancement of Thy kingdom.

Give us the needed strength and grace to help others to hear Thy call. Make it possible for us to send it ringing over land and sea. Purify our lips and lives, that we may be faithful messengers in Thy service.

Pardon us of all sin. Free us from the power of the adversary. Pillow our heads on Thy breast. Keep our eyes fixed on Thy face. Open our ears to hear Thy words. Strengthen our hearts, that we may serve Thee. Help us to say to others, "Come, taste, and see that the Lord is good." Oh, our Father, make us successful in winning souls for Thee. To this end, bless us as we gather together in Thy name. Help us to plan and pray. Keep us, lest we fall away from Thee.

We desire to glorify Thee by a cheerful and hopeful life. We are anxious to merit Thy continued love. Hear us, oh Lord, and answer all our prayers in Thine own way. We ascribe all the praise to Him who has called us and saved us, Jesus Christ, our Redeemer. Amen.

O Thou, supreme Ruler and loving Father, we, the subjects of Thy government and children of Thy household, bow reverently before

Thee, awaiting the gracious benediction of Thy peace. We come to Thee, not in our name, nor through our merit, but in the name of Jesus Christ, Thy Son, and through the merit of His atonement.

Encouraged by Thy loving calls, Thy gracious invitations and precious promises, we come, humbly and penitently, but in the full assurance of faith, with strong desire and confident expectation.

We need not enumerate before Thee our wants, nor plead with Thee for their supply, for Thou knowest all, and art always ready and pleased to give, in abundant measure, to Thy trusting children. But we do pray for the needed preparation to receive with profit what Thou hast in store for us.

Make us, we beseech Thee, more submissive, willing and obedient—more ready to hear and heed Thy loving calls, to accept Thy gracious invitations, and to take into our hearts and lives the rich fullness of grace which Thou art so freely offering. Bless us in our Christian fellowship, and in all the labor of love which our hands find to do. Deliver us from selfishness, pride and jealousy, and enable us, by Thy grace, to walk and work together in love, even as Christ hath loved us and given Himself for us; to Whom, with Thee and the Holy Ghost, ever one God, be all the praise and the glory forever. Amen.

Christ the Light of the World.

✠

RESPONSIVE READING.

Leader. *Glory be to the Father, and to the Son, and to the Holy Ghost.*

Response. As it was in the beginning, is now, and ever shall be world without end. Amen.

L. *Jesus said, I am th light of the world; he that followeth me shal ot walk in darkness, but shall have the light of ʼe. - - -*

R. For with thee is the fountain of life; in thy light shall we see light.

L. *Come ye, and let us walk in the light of the Lord.*

R. For God, who commanded the light to shine out of darkness, hath shined in our hearts, to give the light of the knowledge of the glory of God in the face of Jesus Christ.

L. *Light is sown for the righteous, and gladness for the upright in heart.*

R. The Lord shall be unto thee an everlasting light, and the days of thy mourning shall be ended.

L. *Lord, lift thou up the light of thy countenance upon us.*

R. O send out thy light and thy truth; let
them lead me; let them bring me to thy holy
hill and to thy tabernacles.

L. *Let your light so shine before men that
they may see your good works, and glorify your
Father which is in heaven.*

R. The path of the just is as the shining
light, that shineth more and more unto the perfect day.

L. *Giving thanks unto the Father, who hath
made us meet to be partakers of the inheritance
of the saints in light.*

R. Who hath delivered us from the power
of darkness, and hath translated us into the
kingdom of his dear Son.

L. *Who is the blessed and only Potentate, the
King of kings and Lord of lords, who only hath
immortality, dwelling in the light which no man
can approach unto.*

R. To whom be honor and power everlasting. Amen.

PRAYER.

Most blessed Lord God! Thou eternal fountain of all blessedness and glory—through the
new and living Way we desire to approach
Thee, and offer up our feeble petitions. Power-
less in our own pleadings, we lift up our eyes
to the right-hand of Thy majesty—to that Prince
who ever lives, and "loves, and pleads, and

prays," and always prevails. For His dear
sake, do Thou shine in our souls, dissipate all
clouds of unbelief and sin, empty our hearts of
self, and fill us with love, and holy joy, and
peace. Make one in our midst, we beseech
Thee, at this time, and may we hear Thee saying, "Lo, I am with you always."

O Lord, we pray especially for the coming of
Thy kingdom in the world. Arise, O God, and
let Thine enemies be scattered: gird Thy sword
upon Thy thigh, O Most Mighty, and in Thy
majesty ride prosperously; let Thine arrows be
sharp in the hearts of the King's enemies, until
His sway extends from sea to sea, and from the
river unto the ends of the earth.

We pray for those who have gone forth as
light-bearers to the nations sitting in darkness
and in the shadow of death. May they abide
under Thy almighty protection; may no evil
befall them, nor any plague come nigh their
dwellings. Preserve them from all evil: in
their arduous labors help them, and that right
early. And may hundreds and thousands from
among the heathen shine as stars in their crowns
of rejoicing in the day of the Lord.

We commend ourselves, soul, body, and spirit
to Thy holy keeping. Let us live *near* Thee in
grace, that we may live *with* Thee in glory everlasting. For Jesus' sake we ask it all. And to
Father, Son, and Holy Spirit be ascribed all
praise and glory, world without end. Amen.

ORDER OF SERVICE, No. 12.

Missions.

✠

RESPONSIVE READING.

Leader. *And he said unto them, Go ye into all the world, and preach the Gospel to every creature.*

Response. And they went forth, and preached everywhere, the Lord working with them, and confirming the word with signs following.

L. *Go ye, therefore, and teach all nations, baptizing them in the name of the Father, and of the Son, and of the Holy Ghost:*

R. Teaching them to observe all things whatsoever I have commanded you:

L. *To open their eyes, and to turn them from darkness to light, and the power of Satan unto God.*

R. That they may receive forgiveness of sin, and inheritance among them which are sanctified by faith that is in thee.

L. *How then shall they call on him, in whom they have not believed? And how shall they believe in him, of whom they have not heard? And how shall they hear without a preacher?*

R. And how shall they preach, except they be sent? As it is written, How beautiful are the feet of them that preach the gospel of peace, and bring glad tidings of good things.

All. So then faith cometh by hearing, and hearing by the word of God.

L. *And it sha'l come to pass afterward, that I will pour out my Spirit upon all flesh:*

R. And your sons and your daughters shall prophesy, your old men shall dream dreams, your young men shall see visions.

L. *Then saith he unto his disciples, The harvest truly is plenteous, but the laborers are few;*

R. Pray ye therefore the Lord of the harvest, that he will send forth laborers into his harvest.

PRAYER.

Our Father, we come to Thee in the name of Jesus, feeling our utter unworthiness and helplessness before Thee. O give us the spirit of prayer and supplication. Give us deep humility in Thy holy presence. Help us to come to Thee, asking for just what we want, knowing that Thou wilt supply our need, if we ask aright.

Give us true faith, trust, and confidence in Thee, our Saviour. Help us to come to Thee, as to a dear earthly friend, casting all our care upon Thee, for we know Thou carest for us.

We pray especially now for the cause of Missions everywhere, in our own and in foreign lands. Help the missionaries of the Cross. May they lead many from darkness and ignorance to Thee, the true Light of the world.

Raise up more who will go as missionaries to foreign lands. Inspire many young men with the desire to serve Thee as preachers of the unsearchable riches of Christ. Protect and keep our missionaries in India, in Africa, and in our own country. Give them good health and strength, true faith and trust in Thee, and great success in the work of leading the ignorant and sinful to Jesus.

Prosper the work of our church among the immigrants in the West, where the field is so great, and the laborers so few. Help especially those churches that our Woman's Societies support.

We pray that Thy Holy Spirit may descend on all our churches, so that all the women may become interested in this great work of extending Thy kingdom.

Bless our meeting to-day. Help each one of us to come with a heart full of love to Thee, our Saviour, and desire to serve Thee. Help us all to work and pray for the coming of Thy kingdom on earth.

And when these earthly meetings are over, grant that all of us may meet around Thy throne in heaven, for Jesus' sake. Amen.

———

Dear Heavenly Father, we come to Thee with very thankful hearts that we are permitted to work in Thy vineyard, and we beseech Thee to open our blind eyes and dull hearts to realize that the time is all too short to accomplish what we desire for Thy honor and glory. May we improve every opportunity, and treasure up time and talents for Thy service. We want to realize the preciousness of souls; we want to be filled with burning love and zeal for their salvation. May we, like the great Shepherd of the sheep, *go out* to seek and save the lost, be ready in season and out of season to speak the timely word, to scatter the precious seed, to aid in sending out those who are willing to go out into all the ends of the earth to proclaim Thy glorious Gospel.

May we realize the high and sacred privilege of being co-workers together with God in the salvation of the world. Fire our hearts with the divine ambition of turning many to righteousness. May each one here be a true missionary of the Cross at home and abroad, by prayerful, obedient living, Christ-like temper, gentleness, patience, long-suffering. Make us gladly practice self-denial, to advance the coming of Thy kingdom that is to bring such peace and joy to this weary world, so long cursed by sin. We ask a special blessing on all missionaries who are proclaiming the glad tidings everywhere, especially those of our own beloved household of faith. May they be filled with the Holy Ghost; make the word they preach effectual to the salvation of souls. Comfort and sustain them in every trial. Go before them, and prepare the way; be their rearward, to guard them from evil. May they feel the abiding sense of Thy presence, and be helped by our continual, heartfelt prayers, so that, on the last great day, we all will be enabled to cóme rejoicing into Thy presence, bringing many sheaves gathered out of Thy harvest by our united prayers, offerings, and labors. We ask all in the name of our adorable Redeemer. Amen.

ORDER OF SERVICE, No. 13.

Christian Giving.

The Duty of Giving.

✠

RESPONSIVE READING.

Leader. *Freely ye have received, freely give.*

Response. As we have therefore opportunity, let us do good unto all men: especially unto them who are of the household of faith.

L. *Sell that ye have, and give alms: provide yourselves bags which wax not old, a treasure in the heavens t at faileth not, where no thief approacheth, neither moth corrupteth.*

R. He answered and said unto them, He that hath two coats, let him impart to him that hath none: and he that hath meat, let him do likewise.

L. *Charge them that be ri·h in this world, that they be not high minded, nor trust in uncertain riches, but in the living God, who giveth us richly all things to enjoy:*

R. That they do good, that they be rich in good works, ready to distribute, willing to communicate.

L. *Therefore as ye abound in everything, in faith, and utterance, and knowledge, and in all diligence, and in love to us, see that ye abound in this grace also:*

R. Every man according as he purposeth in his heart, so let him give; not grudgingly, or of necessity.

L. *Upon the first day of the week let every one of you lay by him in store, as God hath prospered him.*

R. But whoso hath this world's goods, and seeth his brother have need, and shutteth up his bowels of compassion from him, how dwelleth the love of God in him?

Blessedness of Giving.

L. *Bring ye all the tithes into the store-house, that there may be meat in mine house,*

R. And prove me now herewith, saith the Lord of hosts, if I will not open you the windows of heaven, and pour you out a blessing, that there shall not be room enough to receive it.

L. *Give, and it shall be given unto you; good measure, pressed down, and shaken together, and running over shall men give into your bosom.*

R. For with the same measure that ye meet withal, it shall be measured to you again.

L. *For this I say, He which soweth sparingly shall reap also sparingly; and he which soweth bountifully shall reap also bountifully.*

R. There is that scattereth and yet increaseth, and there is that withholdeth more than is meet, but it tendeth to poverty.

L. *The liberal soul shall be made fat, and he that watereth shall be watered also himself.*

R. Cast thy bread upon the waters: for thou shalt find it after many days.

L. *He that hath pity upon the poor, lendeth to the Lord, and that which he hath given, will he pay him again.*

R. He hath dispersed abroad; he hath given to the poor; his righteousness remaineth forever.

L. *Honor the Lord with thy substance, and with the first fruits of all thine increase:*

R. So shall thy barns be filled with plenty, and thy presses shall burst out with new wine.

L. *For ye know the grace of the Lord Jesus Christ, that though he was rich, yet for your sakes he became poor, that ye, through his poverty, might be rich.*

R. For the love of Christ constraineth us; and that he died for all, that they which live should not henceforth live unto themselves, but unto him that died for them, and rose again.

PRAYER.

Thou Giver of every good gift, who hast given Thy Son, our Redeemer, in whom we have eternal life, we again give ourselves to Thee. We thank Thee, that we are not in Nature's darkness, but have to guide and inspire us, the light of Thy Word—that the pattern of the Perfect Life makes the path of duty so plain.

We thank Thee for the indwelling of Thy Holy Spirit in our hearts, quickening and warming us as we again gather with new resolve at the cross of our blessed Lord. We give our life to Thee in the joyous service of Thy kingdom, and thank Thee, that we may be laborers together with God. Help us to put away everything that hinders our entire consecration to this great work of spreading the Gospel. Oh, Thou, who was rich, and for our sakes didst become poor, teach us and incline us, and the people among whom we live, to the denial of self, that we grow in giving and in doing day by day. Bless our fellow-laborers in home and in foreign lands, amid their denials and sufferings for the Gospel, and baptize them and us, and all the churches, into the mind of Christ, who gave Himself for us, and for all. Oh, hasten the time when the gold and silver of earth shall be laid on the altar of Christ, when the hearts of Thy professed disciples everywhere shall esteem it their highest joy to live unto Him who died, that we might live forever. We ask all with forgiveness in the name of Jesus, our Lord. Amen.

ORDER OF SERVICE, No. 14.

Christian Love.

✠

CHANT.

Glory be to the Father, and to the Son, and to the Holy Ghost.

As it was in the beginning, is now, and ever shall be, world without end. Amen.

RESPONSIVE READING.

(All standing.)

Leader. *A new commandment I give unto you, That ye love one another; as I have loved you, that ye also love one another.*

Response. By this shall all men know that ye are my disciples, if ye have love one to another.

L. *Be ye kindly affectioned one to another with brotherly love; in honor preferring one another.*

R. Love worketh no ill to his neighbor: therefore love is the fulfilling of the law.

L. *Who shall separate us from the love of Christ?*

R. Shall tribulation, or distress, or persecution, or famine, or nakedness, or peril, or sword?

L. *Let love be without dissimulation. Abhor that which is evil; cleave to that which is good.*

R. But God commendeth his love toward us, in that, while we were yet sinners, Christ died for us.

L. *Behold what manner of love the Father hath bestowed upon us, that we should be called the sons of God!*

R. Therefore the world knoweth us not, because it knew him not.

L. *Beloved, let us love one another, for love is of God; and every one that loveth is born of God, and knoweth God.*

R. He that loveth not knoweth not God: for God is love.

L. *This is the commandment, That, as ye have heard from the beginning, ye should walk in it.*

R. And this is love, that we walk after his commandments.

L. *Jesus answered and said unto him, If a man love me, he will keep my words: and my Father will love him, and we will come unto him, and make our abode with him.*

R. He that loveth me not keepeth not my sayings: and the word which ye hear is not mine, but the Father's which sent me.

L. *That Christ may dwell in your hearts by faith; that ye being rooted and grounded in love.*

R. May be able to comprehend with all saints what is the breadth, and length, and depth, and height;

L. *And to know the love of Christ, which passeth knowledge, that ye might be filled with all the fullness of God.*

R. Be perfect, be of good comfort, be of one mind, live in peace; and the God of love and peace shall be with you.

PRAYER.

Dear Heavenly Father, Thou that hearest and answereth prayer, we come before Thee in all reverence and love, and ask Thy blessing upon us. We thank Thee for all the mercies Thou hast permitted us to enjoy. We are sorry, dear Father, we have come so far short of what Thou didst ask us to measure up to, but we pray Thee to blot out our sins for Jesus' sake, and so fill our hearts with love for Thee and Thy word, that we may become more and more like Thee. Make us to realize so clearly the debt of love we owe, that we may hasten to carry the Gospel message to those who know not the Saviour. Give us that love that suffereth long and is kind, that thinketh no evil, that will make us more eager to do Thy bidding; the love that will make us thoughtful of Thy poor, whom we have always with us; may we be ever ready to minister to their needs.

Thou hast taught us, O God, to love one another with a pure heart, to be pitiful, to be courteous, to love even as Christ loved us: grant that we may love in deed and truth, and so fulfill the law of Christ. We ask Thy blessing on our society and all the work we may undertake in Thy name. May we be ready with our means and our prayers to help those who are in far-off lands preaching the Gospel: bless those who are laboring at home. Be with us, as we go our way in the world, and give us that perfect love that casteth out fear. All this we ask f r His sake, who loved us, and gave Himself for us. Amen.

ORDER OF SERVICE, No. 15.

Joyous Service.

✠

RESPONSIVE READING.

Leader. *What shall I render unto the Lord for all his benefits toward me?*

Response. Sing unto him, sing psalms unto him; talk ye of all his wondrous works. Glory ye in his holy name: let the heart of them rejoice that seek the Lord.

L. *Let the heavens be glad, and let the earth rejoice, and let men say among the nations, The Lord reigneth.*

R. Whom having not seen, ye love; in whom, though now ye see him not, yet believing, ye rejoice with joy unspeakable and full of glory.

L. *Glory ye in his holy name; let the heart of them rejoice that seek the Lord.*

R. Blessed is the people that know the joyful sound; they shall walk, O Lord, in the light of thy countenance.

L. *I was glad when they said unto me, Let us go into the house of the Lord.*

R. My meditation of him shall be sweet.

L. *Serve the Lord with gladness, come before his presence with singing.*

R. Let all those that put their trust in thee rejoice: let them ever shout for joy, because thou defendeth them: let them also that love thy name be joyful in thee.

L. *Because thou servedst not the Lord thy God with joyfulness, and with gladness of heart, for the abundance of all things; therefore shalt thou serve thine enemies.*

R. It is joy to the just to do judgment.

L. *Serve the Lord with gladness.*

R. And the seventy returned again with joy, saying, Lord, even the devils are subject unto us through thy name.

L. *I have spoken to you, that my joy might remain in you, and that your joy may be full.*

R. I will be glad and rejoice in thee: I will sing praise to thy name, O thou Most High.

L. *Let the righteous be glad; let them rejoice before God: yea, let them exceedingly rejoice.*

R. I have longed for thy salvation, O Lord, and thy law is my delight.

L. *Rejoice in the Lord always: and again I say, Rejoice.*

PRAYER.

We thank Thee, our Heavenly Father, for all the hope and all the gladness that are revealed through Jesus Christ, our Lord. We thank Thee that we are not called to a life of sorrow, but out of sorrow to a life of joy. Thou hast given us not only the necessities of life, but so many things which add to our pleasure; but we realize that these things perish with the using, while the joy Thou hast laid up in store for us will endure forever.

Our Father, we rejoice in the revelation of Thyself as the tender, loving Father. That, like as a father pitieth his children, so the Lord pitieth them that fear Him. We rejoice daily that we are children of such a Father, who knoweth our every thought, even before it is uttered, and who is more willing to give, than we are to ask. Grant Thy presence to-day. May all recognize it with them as a thought, as a hope, as an inspiration, or as a power. May we feel the touch of God upon the soul, awakening it to the thought of broader life in nearness to God. We find the purest joy of life is nearness to Thee, and it is only where Thy light and love have come on earth that true and pure joy exists. Wilt Thou have compassion upon all those who know Thee not. Help us to spread the blessings of gospel knowledge to those that are without it. Make this land and the lands of the earth to be the habitation of righteousness.

We rejoice that Thou hast called us to Thy service. May it be our meat to do Thy will.

The whole earth is vocal with Thy praise, the heavens declare Thy glory, and the hills rejoice together. Hasten the time, O Lord, when the nations of the earth shall rejoice in Thy knowledge, and every creature shall magnify Thy name, and to Thee shall be all praise and rejoicing forevermore. Amen.

ORDER OF SERVICE, No. 16.

Constraining Grace

✠

CHANT.

Glory be to the Father, and to the Son, and to the Holy Ghost.

As it was in the beginning, is now, and ever shall be, world without end. Amen.

RESPONSIVE READING.

(*All standing.*)

Leader. *Ye know the grace of our Lord Jesus Christ, that, though he was rich, yet for your sakes he became poor, that ye through his poverty might become rich.*

Response. Whom having not seen, we love.

L. *Whatsoever we do, let us do it heartily, as to the Lord.*

R. For the love of Christ constraineth us.

L. *Jesus said, I am the bread of life: he that cometh to me shall never hunger, and he that believeth on me shall never thirst.*

R. Lord, evermore give us this bread.

L. *Jesus said, If any man will come after me, let him deny himself, and take up his cross, and follow me.*

R. Lord I will follow thee whithersoever thou goest.

L. *Put on, therefore, as the elect of God, holy and beloved, bowels of mercies, kindness, humbleness of mind, meekness, long-suffering; forbearing one another, and forgiving one another: even as Christ forgave you.*

R. Behold, what manner of love the Father hath bestowed upon us, that we should be called the sons of God!

L. *Jesus said, Go ye, therefore, and teach all nations.*

R. Looking for that blessed hope, and the glorious appearing of the great God and our Saviour Jesus Christ.

L. *Behold, I come quickly; and my reward is with me, to give every man according as his work shall be.*

R. Amen. Even so come. Lord Jesus.

PRAYER.

We come to Thee, our Heavenly Father, with hearts full of rejoicing. Thy goodness does not fail. Thou art always the same, and dost bear Thyself towards us with paternal love.

We thank Thee, our Father, for the grace that has called us from darkness to light. We rejoice in the blessings that have come to us in our Christian life. We thank Thee for our homes, our churches, our Bibles, our schools, our friends; for our missionary societies, and for every agency that is at work to save the lost.

Teach us, O God, how constantly we depend upon Thee, and how we are kept in our places, steadfast in our work, by Thy grace. Without Thee, we can do nothing.

It is of Thy grace that we are restrained from evil. Throw about us, our Father, Thy constant safeguards. Make us watchful against the evils that are about us and beset us on every hand. Keep us from indifference to the great interests which are always before us in the church.

Make our lives to abound in good, that the work of Thy restraining grace may be accomplished easily in each one of us, that we receive not the grace of God in vain.

Prosper, O Lord, the work before us; increase the number of the workers. Open to us new doors of usefulness. Remember very graciously those whom we have sent into distant fields, and all whom we send into our home field. Prosper their work. Comfort the solitary. Bring in those who are without the fold, and may we see the work of the Lord prosper in our hands.

These things we ask, our Father, with all else that we need, through Jesus Christ, our Lord. Amen.

ORDER OF SERVICE, No. 17.

Worship.

✠

RESPONSIVE READING.

(*All standing.*)

Leader. *O come, let us worship and bow down; let us kneel before the Lord our Maker.*

Response. All nations whom thou hast made shall come and worship before thee, O Lord.

L. *The dark places of the earth are full of the habitations of cruelty.*

R. The Lord hath done great things for *us;* whereof we are glad.

L. *Blessed be the Lord, who daily loadeth us with benefits.*

R. What shall I render unto the Lord for all his benefits toward me ?

L. *Declare his glory among the heathen, his wonders among all people.*

R. I will speak of the glorious honor of thy majesty and of thy wondrous works.

L. *The Lord gave the word; great was the company of those that published it.*

R. His word runneth very swiftly.

L. *Pray for the peace of Jerusalem.*

R. Hearken unto the voice of my cry, **my King,** and my God: for unto thee will I pray.

L. *I will offer to thee the sacrifice of thanksgiving, I will pay my vows unto the Lord now, in the presence of all his people.*

R. The Lord remember all thy offerings and accept thy burnt sacrifice.

L. *All the ends of the world shall remember and turn unto the Lord; and all the kindreds of the nations shall worship before thee.*

R. Princes shall come out of Egypt; Ethiopia shall soon stretch out her hands unto God.

L. *He shall have dominion also from sea to sea, and from the river to the ends of the earth.*

R. Yea, all kings shall fall down before him; all nations shall serve him.

L. *Blessed be his glorious name forever, and let the whole earth be filled with his glory.*

R. Lift up your heads, O ye gates; even lift them up, ye everlasting doors; and the King of glory shall come in.

L. *Let us pray.*

PRAYER.

Father in heaven, we come before Thee this day with humility, because Thou art the great and holy God who dost rule over nations, and we are of the earth and like the earth, and are not fit to come into Thy presence. And yet we come with boldness and joy, for Thou art our

Father and we Thy children; and we know Thou wilt accept us through Jesus, and hear and answer us.

May Thy Holy Spirit come now into each heart, and fill our souls with devotion to Thee, and with Thy love, the love Thou hast to all men; and may we from this hour live not unto ourselves, but unto Thee, and lay down our lives for the brethren, even as Thou hast shewed us in Thy word, and as Thou dost direct us day by day.

Thou hast done so much for us, Lord Jesus, we would do something for Thee, and Thou art so good as to let us have a share in the work of saving souls. We pray Thee to keep us at Thy feet listening always to Thy words, that we be not left to serve alone. Give us wisdom and zeal to do Thy work in Thy way. Make us more and more like Jesus, who went about doing good.

Show to those who care not for Thy kingdom, the duty and the joy of service, that many more laborers may enter into Thy vineyard. O, may the day soon come, when all shall know and love Thee, when the crowns of all nations shall be laid at Thy feet, and Thou shalt come into Thy kingdom.

We would prepare the way for Thy coming; we would open wide the gates and doors, that the King of glory may come in to every heart Even so come, Lord Jesus. Amen.

ORDER OF SERVICE, No. 18.

Prayer and Promises.

✠

RESPONSIVE READING.

Leader. *Lord, bow down thine ear and hear; open, Lord, thine eyes, and see.*

Response. The eyes of the Lord are upon the righteous, and his ears are open to their cry.

L. *For thy name's sake lead me, and guide me.*

R. The Lord shall guide thee continually.

L. *Hold thou me up, and I shall be safe.*

R. I will uphold thee with the right hand of my righteousness.

L. *Order my steps in thy word.*

R. The steps of a good man are ordered by the Lord.

L. *Lead me, O Lord, in thy righteousness, make thy way straight before my face.*

R. I will lead them in paths that they have not known: I will make crooked things straight.

L. *Search me, O God, and know my heart; try me, and know my thoughts.*

R. I the Lord search the heart, I try the reins.

L. *I have gone astray like a lost sheep: seek thy servant.*

R. Thus saith the Lord God, I will both search my sheep, and seek them out.

L. *If thy presence go not with me, carry us not up hence.*

R. My presence shall go with thee, and I will give thee rest.

L. *Oh, that thou wouldst keep me from evil.*

R. The Lord is faithful, who shall keep you from evil.

L. *O Lord, let thy loving kindness and thy truth continually preserve me.*

R. The Lord preserveth all them that love him.

L. *Lord, increase our faith.*

R. Believe in the Lord your God, so shall ye be established.

L. *O that I might have my request; and tha. God would grant me the thing I long for.*

R. Delight thyself in the Lord, and he shal give thee the desires of thine heart.

L. *Abide with us.*

R. The Father shall give you another Com forter, that he may abide with you forever

PRAYER.

Dear Father, we come unto Thee, feeling our great weakness, and constant need of Thee.

.

Have mercy upon us, O God, according to Thy loving kindness: according unto the multitude of Thy tender mercies, blot out all our transgressions. Fulfill unto us the desires and petitions of our hearts, while we kneel before Thee. Help us each to seek first the kingdom of heaven and His righteousnees, resting fully upon Thy promise, that all other necessary things shall be added to these.

Dear Father, grant us each a deeper, abiding love to Christ, that it may pervade and influence all our deeds. Grant unto us grace, and wisdom to perform acceptably the work Thou hast laid upon us as Thy children. Awaken in us a deep conviction of the greatness of our privileges, and remind us constantly, that to whom much is given, of him will much be required. Constrain us, by the love of Christ, to do Thy will, and walk in all Thy ways. Bless, we pray Thee, all agencies at work for bringing the world to Christ. Hasten the day when all nations, kindreds, and tongues, shall rejoice in His name, and crown Him Lord of all.

Dear Father, accept and answer our prayer, which we leave at Thy throne, without a doubt of Thy love and willingness to receive and bless, through Jesus Christ, our Lord, to whom be glory, and honor, and power forever. Amen.

ORDER OF SERVICE, No. 19.

A Christian Nation.

✠

RESPONSIVE READING

Leader. *Blessed is the nation whose God is the Lord.*

Response. For the nation and kingdom that will not serve the Lord shall perish : yea, those nations shall be utterly wasted.

L. *Righteousness exalteth a nation: but sin is a reproach to any people.*

R. If thou shalt hearken diligently unto the voice of the Lord thy God, to observe and to do all his commandments which I command thee this day, that the Lord thy God will set thee on high, above all the nations of the earth.

L. *Ye shall be my people, and I will be your God.*

R. They seek me daily, and delight to know my ways, as a nation that did righteousness, and forsook not the ordinance of their God: they ask of me the ordinances of justice; they take delight in approaching to God.

L. *Open ye the gates, that the righteous nation which keepeth the truth may enter in.*

R. Thou hast increased the nation, O Lord, thou hast increased the nation; thou art glorified.

L. *And what one nation in the earth is like thy people.*

R. Ye are a chosen generation, a royal priesthood, a holy nation, a peculiar people: that ye should show forth the praises of him who hath called you out of darkness into his marvellous light.

L. *Obey my voice, and I will be your God, and ye shall be my people; and walk ye in all the ways that I have commanded you, that it may be well unto you.*

R. Thy people also shall be all righteous; they shall inherit the land forever: thy sun shall no more go down: neither shall thy moon withdraw itself; for the Lord shall be thine everlasting light.

L. *Hearken unto me, my people; and give ear unto me, O my nation: for a law shall proceed from me, and I will make my judgment to rest for a light of the people.*

R. I have put my words in thy mouth, and I have covered thee in the shadow of mine hand, that I may plant the heavens, and lay the foundations of the earth, and say unto Zion. Thou art my people.

PRAYER.

Oh, Lord, our Heavenly Father, Thou art a God of order, and not a God of confusion. By

Thee kings reign and princes decree justice. Thou hast been pleased to give us our homes in this land of peace and prosperity. Thou hast given us fruitful fields and abundant harvests, and hast rewarded the useful labors of all our people. For Thy great goodness we devoutly thank Thee. Thou hast fed us and clothed us and kept us from evil. We earnestly invoke Thy blessing upon our country. Make us wholly a Christian nation. Thou hast set us in this land as a chosen people, Thou hast prospered our rulers, Thou hast made us a free and a mighty people. Give us, we pray Thee, - a sense of our responsibility to Thee, and to the world, and keep us a nation to serve only Thee. May we not be given over to wordly lusts and aims, but let us understand that, except we build for Thee, we build in vain, and must perish from the earth. Grant, then, that this land and this nation be wholly given to Thee; let our prosperity all be turned to Thy service; let justice, peace and true godliness be the foundations of our national life, and may we be known throughout all lands as a nation where God reigns. We pray Thee, O God, that we may as a people labor for the upbuilding of Thy kingdom everywhere, and that we may show before all the world that we become wise as we become great, and that our wisdom is from Thee; may we, through Thy service, and through Thy wise counselings, and our hearkening thereto, become unto other nations as a beacon-light, whereby ignorance and error shall be guided into truth and righteousness. May the people of other lands who seek us receive of us spiritual enrichment and enlightenment; and as our own people go hence into stranger lands, may it be as a dispersion of the disciples of Jesus Christ spreading abroad the glory of the Lord. We ask, O Lord, especially that Thou wilt help us to destroy our national evils. Make us strong to war against all corruption, and intemperance, and all vice of every kind which threatens our national life; help us to uproot every evil, and let every citizen of this great republic be filled with that sublime patriotism that brands sin as treason to his country.

Lord, we have prayed unto Thee for this Thy people. Go Thou before them as Supreme Guide and Ruler, until the kingdoms of the earth shall become Thy kingdom, and Thy will be wholly done among us. We ask it all in the name of Jesus Christ. Amen.

ORDER OF SERVICE, No. 20.

Thanksgiving.

✠

RESPONSIVE READING.

Leader. *O give thanks unto the Lord; for he is good:*

Response. For his mercy endureth forever.

L. *Give thanks unto the Lord, call upon his name, make known his deeds among the people.*

R. Glory ye in his holy name: let the heart of them rejoice that seek the Lord.

L. *Come before his presence with thanksgiving.*

R. Let us worship and bow down: let us kneel before the Lord our Maker.

L. *It is a good thing to give thanks unto the Lord, and to sing praises unto t y name, O Most High.*

R. To show forth thy loving kindness in the morning. and thy faithfulness every night.

L. *Let my prayer be set forth before thee as incense; and the lifting up of my hands as the evening sacrifice.*

R. In everything by prayer and supplication with thanksgiving let your request be made known unto the Lord.

L. *Surely the righteous shall give thanks unto thy name: the upright shall dwell in thy presence.*

R. Declare his glory among the heathen, his wonders among all people.

L. *Enter into his gates with thanksgiving: and into his courts with praise:*

R. Be thankful unto him, and bless his name.

L. *O let the nations be glad and sing for joy: for thou shalt judge the people righteously, and govern the nations upon earth.*

R. God shall bless us; and all the ends of the earth shall fear him.

PRAYER.

O Lord, our God, Thou hast opened Thy hands, and the earth is filled with the abundance of Thy blessings. Thou art the source of all good, and all blessings. both temporal and spiritual, are from Thee.

May Thy Holy Spirit so enlighten our minds that we may recognize Thy mercies all about us. The air we breathe, the food we eat, our homes, and our dear ones are all gifts from Thee. It is in Thee we live, move, and have our being. We thank Thee, our Heavenly Father, that the lines have fallen to us in pleasant places, and that ours is a goodly heritage. Thy mercies are new every morning, and Thy faithfulness every night.

Day unto day uttereth speech, and night unto night showeth knowledge. Thou art dispelling the darkness of heathen lands. Thy praise shall be among the nations.

Help us, O our Father, to praise Thee with our whole hearts, and to show forth all Thy marvellous works Thy loving kindnesses have been ever of old, and Thy tender mercies are over all Thy works. We thank Thee for all our blessed privileges and opportunities. We thank Thee for the revelation of Thy will in the Bible, and for the gift of Thy dear Son, our Saviour, and for the guidance of the Holy Spirit to lead us in the way of truth. We pray Thee, dear Father, that our lives may be living songs of praise and thanksgiving, that, when we are through with praises here, we may be prepared to join with the hosts who shall praise Thee, world without end. Amen.

HYMNS.

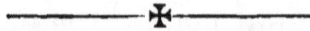

OPENING HYMNS.

1   CHANT.

Glory be to the Father, and to the Son,
  And to the Holy Ghost,
As it was in the beginning,
  Is now, and ever shall be,
World without end. Amen.

2   CHANT.

Our Father, who art in Heaven,
  Hallowed be thy name:
Thy kingdom come,
  Thy will be done on earth,
As it is in heaven;
Give us this day our daily bread;
  And forgive us our trespasses,
As we forgive them that
  Trespass against us.
And lead us not into temptation,
  But deliver us from evil;
For thine is the kingdom,
  The power and the glory,
Forever. Amen.

3   8s 7s & 4s

1. In Thy name, O Lord, assembling,
  We, Thy people, now draw near:
Teach us to rejoice with trembling;
  Speak, and let Thy servants hear:
    Hear with meekness—
Hear Thy word with godly fear.

2. While our days on earth are lengthen'd
     May we give them, Lord, to Thee:
   Cheer'd by hope, and daily strengthen'd,
     May we run, nor weary be,
       Till Thy glory
   Without cloud in heaven we see.

3. There, in worship purer, sweeter,
     All Thy people shall adore;
   Tasting of enjoyment greater
     Than they could conceive before;
       Full enjoyment,
   Full and pure forevermore.

4 C. M.

1. In Thy great name, O Lord, we come,
     To worship at Thy feet;
   Oh, pour Thy Holy Spirit down
     On all that now shall meet.

2. We come to hear Jehovah speak,
     To hear the Saviour's voice;
   Thy face and favor, Lord, we seek,
     Now make our hearts rejoice.

3. Teach us to pray and praise, and hear
     And understand Thy word:
   To feel Thy blissful presence near,
     And trust our living Lord.

5 L. M.

1. Where two or three with sweet accord,
   Obedient to their sovereign Lord,
   Meet to recount His acts of grace,
   And offer solemn prayer and praise—

2. "There," says the Saviour, "will I be,
   Amid this little company:
   To them unveil My smiling face,
   And shed My glories round the place."

3. We meet at Thy command, dear Lord,
   Relying on Thy faithful word:

Now send Thy Spirit from above,
Now fill our hearts with heavenly love.

6   H. M.

1. O Thou that hearest prayer!
    Attend our humble cry;
And let Thy servants share
    Thy blessing from on high;
We plead the promise of Thy word.
Grant us Thy Holy Spirit, Lord!

2· If earthly parents hear
    Their children when they cry;
If they, with love sincere,
    Their children's wants supply,
Much more wilt Thou Thy love display
And answer when Thy children pray.

3. Our heavenly Father, Thou;
    We, children of Thy grace:
Oh, let Thy Spirit now
    Descend and fill the place,
That all may feel the heavenly flame,
And all unite to praise Thy name.

7   L. M.

1. Come, Saviour Jesus, from above,
    Assist me with Thy heavenly grace;
Empty my heart of earthly love,
    And for Thyself prepare the place.

2. Oh, let Thy sacred presence fill
    And set my longing spirit free,
Which pants to have no other will,
    But night and day to feast on Thee.

3. Henceforth may no profane delight
    Divide this consecrated soul;
Possess it Thou, who hast the right,
    As Lord and Master of the whole.

4. Nothing on earth do I desire,
    But Thy pure love within my breast;
This, only this, will I require,
    And freely give up all the rest.

8   C. M.

1. Come, Holy Spirit, heavenly Dove,
    With all Thy quickening powers,
Kindle a flame of sacred love
    In these cold hearts of ours.

2. See how we grovel here below,
    Fond of these earthly toys;
Our souls how heavily they go
    To reach eternal joys.

3. Dear Lord, and shall we always live
    At this poor dying rate?
Our love so cold, so faint to Thee,
    And Thine to us so great?

4. Come, Holy Spirit, heavenly Dove,
    With all Thy quickening powers;
Come, shed abroad a Saviour's love,
    And that shall kindle our's.

9   7s.

1. Holy Ghost, with light divine,
Shine upon this heart of mine!
Chase the shades of night away,
Turn the darkness into day.

2. Let me see my Saviour's face,
Let me all His beauties trace;
Show those glorious truths to me,
Which are only known to Thee.

3. Holy Ghost, with power divine,
Cleanse this guilty heart of mine;
Long has sin, without control,
Held dominion o'er my soul.

4. Holy Ghost, with joy divine,
   Cheer this sadden'd heart of mine;
   Bid my many woes depart,
   Heal my wounded, bleeding heart.

10   S. M.

1. Come. Holy Spirit, come;
   Let Thy bright beams arise:
   Dispel the sorrow from our minds,
   The darkness from our eyes.

2. Convince us all of sin,
   Then lead to Jesus' blood,
   And to our wondering view reveal
   The mercies of our God.

3. Revive our drooping faith,
   Our doubts and fears remove,
   And kindle in out breasts the flame
   Of never-dying love.

11   C. M.

1. Come, thou Fount of every blessing,
   Tune my heart to sing Thy grace;
   Streams of mercy, never ceasting,
   Call for songs of loudest praise;
   Teach me some melodious measure,
   Sung by flaming tongues above;
   Fill my soul with sacred pleasure,
   While I sing redeeming love.

2. Here I raise my Ebenezer,
   Hither by Thy help I've come,
   And I hope, by Thy good pleasure,
   Safely to arrive at home.
   Jesus sought me when a stranger,
   Wandering from the fold of God,
   He, to save my soul from danger,
   Interposed His precious blood.

3. Oh, to grace how great a debtor
   Daily I'm constrained to be!

Let that grace, Lord, like a fetter,
  Bind my wandering heart to Thee!
Prone to wonder, Lord, I feel it;
  Prone to leave the God I love—
Here's my heart, Lord, take and seal it,
  Seal it for Thy courts above.

---

12   **PRAISE.**   8s 7s.

1. All hail the power of Jesus' name,
    Let angels prostrate fall:
  Bring forth the royal diadem,
    And crown Him Lord of all.

2. Crown Him, ye martyrs of our God,
    Who from His altar call:
  Extol the stem of Jesse's rod,
    And crown Him Lord of all.

3. Ye chosen seed of Israel's race,
    A remnant weak and small,
  Hail Him who saves you by His grace,
    And crown Him Lord of all.

4. Ye gentile sinners, ne'er forget
    The wormwood and the gall;
  Go, spread your trophies at His feet,
    And crown Him Lord of all.

5. Let every kindred, every tribe,
    On this terrestrial ball,
  To Him all majesty ascribe,
    And crown Him Lord of all.

6. Oh, that with yonder sacred throng,
    We at His feet may fall!
  We'll join the everlasting song,
    And crown Him Lord of all.

13

1. Holy, Holy, Holy! Lord God Almighty!
   Early in the morning our songs shall rise
       to Thee;
   Holy, Holy Holy! Merciful and mighty!
   God in Three Persons, blessed Trinity!

2. Holy, Holy, Holy! All the saints adore Thee,
   Casting down their golden crowns around
       the glassy sea;
   Cherubim and Seraphim falling down before
       Thee,
   Which wert, and art, and evermore shalt be.

3. Holy, Holy, Holy! Tho' the darkness hide
       Thee,
   Though the eye of sinful man Thy glory
       may not see,
   Only Thou art Holy, there is none beside
       Thee,
   Perfect in pow'r, in love and purity.

4. Holy, Holy, Holy! Lord God Almighty!
   All Thy works shall praise Thy name, in
       earth, and sky, and sea;
   Holy, Holy, Holy! Merciful and Mighty!
   God in Three Persons, blessed Trinity!

14   L. M.

1. Before Jehovah's awful throne,
   Ye nations, bow with sacred joy;
   Know that the Lord is God alone:
   He can create, and He destroy.

2. His sov'reign power, without our aid,
   Made us of clay, and form'd us men,
   And, when like wand'ring sheep we stray'd,
   He brought us to His fold again.

3. We'll crowd Thy gates with thankful songs,
   High as the heavens our voices raise:
   And earth, with her ten thousand tongues,
   Shall fill Thy courts with sounding praise

4. Wide as the world is Thy command;
   Vast as eternity Thy love;
   Firm as a rock Thy truth must stand,
   When rolling years shall cease to move.

15   7s.

1. God of mercy, God of grace,
   Show the brightness of Thy face:
   Shine upon us, Saviour! shine;
   Fill Thy Church with light divine;
   And Thy saving health extend
   To the earth's remotest end.

2. Let the people praise Thee. Lord!
   Be by all that live adored:
   Let the nations shout and sing
   Glory to their Saviour King!
   At Thy feet their tribute pay,
   And Thy holy will obey.

3. Let the people praise Thee, Lord!
   Earth shall then her fruits afford;
   God to man His blessings give,
   Man to God devoted live;
   All below and all above,
   One in joy and light and love.

16   10s 11s.

1. Oh, worship the King all glorious above,
   Oh! gratefully sing his power and love,
   Our Shield and Defender, the Ancient of days,
   Pavilioned in splendor, and girded with
        praise.

2. Oh, tell of His might, Oh! sing of His grace,
   Whose robe is the light, whose canopy space!

His chariots of wrath the deep thunder-clouds
    form,
And dark is His path on the wings of the
    storm.

3. Thy bountiful care what tongue can recite!
It breathes in the air, it shine in the light;
It streams from the hills, it descends to the
    plain,
And sweetly distils in the dew and the rain.

5. Frail children of dust, and feeble as frail,
In Thee do we trust, nor find Thee to fail;
Thy mercies how tender, How firm to the end,
Our Maker, Defender, Redeemer and Friend.

17   C. M.

1. Oh, for a heart to praise my God,
    A heart from sin set free:
A heart that always feels Thy blood
    So freely spilt for me.

2. A heart resigned, submissive, meek,
    My great Redeemer's throne:
Where only Christ is heard to speak,
    Where Jesus reigns alone.

3. Oh, for a lowly, contrite heart,
    Believing, true, and clean:
Which neither life nor death can part
    From Him that dwells within.

4. A heart in every thought renewed,
    And full of love divine;
Perfect, and right, and pure, and good,
    A copy, Lord, of Thine.

18   C. M.

1. Oh, for a thousand tongues to sing
    My dear Redeemer's praise;
The glories of my God and King,
    The triumphs of His grace!

2. My gracious Master and my God,
   Assist me to proclaim.
   To spread through all the earth abroad
   The honors of Thy name.

3. Jesus, the name that calms our fears,
   That bids our sorrows cease;
   'Tis music in the sinner's ears:
   'Tis life, and health, and peace.

4. He breaks the power of reigning sin,
   He sets the prisoner free;
   His blood can make the foulest clean;
   His blood availed for me.

19

1. Crown Him with many crowns,
   The Lamb upon His throne;
   Hark. how the heav'nly anthem drowns
   All music but its own;
   Awake, my soul, and sing
   Of Him who died for thee.
   And hail Him as thy matchless King
   Thro' all eternity.

2. Crown Him the Lord of love: .
   Behold His hands and side,
   Rich wounds yet visible above
   In beauty glorified:
   No angel in the sky
   Can fully bear that sight,
   But downward bends his burning eye
   At mysteries so great.

3. Crown Him the Lord of peace:
   Whose pow'r a scepter sways
   From pole to pole. that wars may cease,
   And all be pray'r and praise:
   His reign shall know no end,
   And round His pierced feet
   Fair flow'rs of Paradise extend
   Their fragrance ever sweet.

4. Crown Him the Lord of years,
The Potentate of time,
Creator of the rolling spheres,
Ineffably sublime.
Allhail, Redeemer, hail!
For Thou hast died for me;
Thy praise shall never, never fail
Throughout eternity.

20   6s, 4s.

1. Come, Thou almighty King,
Help us Thy name to sing,
Help us to praise!
Father all glorious,
O'er all victorious,
Come and reign over us,
Ancient of days.

2. Jesus, our Lord, descend;
From all our foes defend,
Nor let us fall:
Let Thine almighty aid
Our sure defence be made,
Our souls on Thee be stay'd;
Lord, hear our call!

3. Come, holy Comforter,
Thy sacred witness bear,
In this glad hour:
Thou, who almighty art,
Now rule in every heart,
And ne'er from us depart,
Spirit of power.

4. To Thee, great One in Three,
The highest praises be,
Hence evermore!
Thy sov'reign majesty
May we in glory see,
And to eternity
Love and adore!

Hymns of Faith and Hope.

21   6s, 4s.

1. My faith looks up to Thee,
   Thou Lamb of Calvary,
       Saviour divine!
   Now hear me while I pray,
   Take all my guilt away,
   Oh, let me from this day
       Be wholly Thine!

2. May Thy rich grace impart
   Strength to my fainting heart,
       My zeal inspire!
   As Thou hast died for me,
   Oh, may my love to Thee,
   Pure, warm, and changeless be,
       A living fire.

3. While life's dark maze I tread,
   And griefs around me spread,
       Be Thou my guide;
   Bid darkness turn to day,
   Wipe sorrow's tears away,
   Nor let me ever stray
       From Thee aside.

4. When ends life's transient dream,
   When death's cold, sullen stream
       Shall o'er me roll:
   Blest Saviour, then, in love,
   Fear and distrust remove,
   Oh, bear me safe above,
       A ransomed soul.

22   7s.

1. Jesus, Lover of my soul,
       Let me to Thy bosom fly,
   While the nearer waters roll,
       While the tempest still is high:

Hide me, O my Saviour, hide,
  Till the storm of life is past;
Safe into the haven guide:
  Oh, receive my soul at last!

2. Other refuge have I none;
  Hangs my helpless soul on Thee:
Leave, ah, leave me not alone,
  Still support and comfort me:
All my trust on Thee is stay'd,
  All my help from Thee I bring;
Cover my defenceless head
  With the shadow of Thy wing.

3. Thou, O Christ, art all I want;
  More than all in Thee I find:
Raise the fallen, cheer the faint,
  Heal the sick, and lead the blind.
Just and holy is Thy name;
  I am all unrighteousness;
False and full of sin I am;
  Thou art full of truth and grace.

4. Plenteous grace with Thee is found,
  Grace to cover all my sin;
Let the healing streams abound,
  Make and keep me pure within.
Thou of life the Fountain art,
  Freely let me take of Thee:
Spring Thou up within my heart,
  Rise to all eternity.

23   6s & 4s

1. Nearer, my God, to Thee,
  Nearer to Thee!
E'en though it be a cross
  That raiseth me;
Still all my song shall be,
Nearer, my God, to Thee,
  Nearer to Thee!

2. Though like a wanderer,
   The sun gone down,
Darkness be over me,
   My rest a stone;
Yet in my dreams I'd be
Nearer, my God, to Thee,
   Nearer to Thee.

3. There let the way appear
   Steps unto heaven,
All that Thou sendest me
   In mercy given;
Angels to beckon me
Nearer, my God, to Thee.
   Nearer to Thee!

4. Then with my waking thoughts
   Bright with Thy praise,
Out of my stony griefs
   Bethel I'll raise;
So by my woes to be
Nearer, my God, to Thee,
   Nearer to Thee.

5. Or if on joyful wing,
   Cleaving the sky,
Sun, moon, and stars forgot,
   Upwards I fly,
Still all my song shall be,
Nearer, my God, to Thee,
   Nearer to Thee!

24   7s.

1. Take my life and let it be
Consecrated, Lord, to Thee;
Take my hands and let them move
At the impulse of Thy love.
All to Thee, all to Thee,
Consecrated, Lord, to Thee.

2. Take my feet and let them be
   Swift and beautiful for Thee;
   Take my voice and let me sing
   Always, only for my King.
   All to Thee, all to Thee,
   Consecrated, Lord, to Thee.

3. Take my lips and let them be
   Fill'd with messages from Thee!
   Take my silver and my gold,
   Not a mite would I withhold.
   All to Thee, all to Thee.
   Consecrated, Lord, to Thee.

4. Take my moments and my days,
   Let them flow in endless praise;
   Take my intellect and use
   Ev'ry pow'r as Thou shalt choose.
   All to Thee, all to Thee,
   Consecrated, Lord, to Thee.

5. Take my will and make it Thine,
   It shall be no longer mine:
   Take my heart, it is Thine own,
   It shall be Thy royal throne.
   All to Thee, all to Thee,
   Consecrated, Lord, to Thee.

6. Take my love, my God, I pour
   At Thy feet its treasure store:
   Take myself, and I will be
   Ever, only, all for Thee.
   All for Thee, all for Thee,
   Consecrated, Lord, to Thee.

25   L. M.

1. So let our lips and lives express
   The holy gospel we profess;
   So let our works and virtues shine,
   To prove the doctrine all divine!

2. Thus shall we best proclaim abroad
The honors of our Saviour, God,
When the salvation reigns within,
And grace subdues the power of sin.

3. Our flesh and sense must be denied,
Passion and envy, lust and pride;
While justice, temperance, truth and love
Our inward piety approve.

4. Religion bears our spirits up,
Whilst we expect that blessed hope,
The bright appearance of the Lord,
And faith stands leaning on His word,

26
7s.

1. Rock of Ages! cleft for me,
Let me hide myself in Thee!
Let the water and the blood,
From Thy riven side that flowed,
Be of sin the double cure:
Save me, Lord, and make me pure

2. Not the labors of my hands
Can fulfil Thy law's demands:
Could my zeal no respite know,
Could my tears forever flow,
All for sin could not atone:
Thou must save, and Thou alone!

3. Nothing in my hand I bring,
Simply to Thy cross I cling;
Naked, come to Thee for dress:
Helpless, look to Thee for grace;
Foul, I to the Fountain fly:
Wash me, Saviour, or I die!

4. While I draw this fleeting breath,
When mine eyelids close in death,
When I soar through tracts unknown,

See Thee on Thy judgement throne,—
Rock of Ages! cleft for me,
Let me hide myself in Thee!

27   8s, 7s & 4.

1. Guide me, O Thou great Jehovah!
     Pilgrim through this barren land;
   I am weak, but Thou art mighty,
     Hold me with Thy powerful hand:
   Bread of heaven,
     Feed me till I want no more.

2. Open Thou the crystal fountain
     Whence the healing streams do flow:
   Let the fiery, cloudy pillar
     Lead me all my journey through:
   Strong Deliv'rer,
     Be Thou still my Strength and Shield.

3. When I tread the verge of Jordan,
     Bid my anxious fears subside;
   Death of death! and hell's Destruction!
     Land me safe on Canaan's side:
   Songs of praises
     I will ever give to Thee.

28   7s, 6s.

1. Jerusalem, the golden,
     With milk and honey blest!
   Beneath thy contemplation
     Sink heart and voice oppressed:
   I know not, oh, I know not,
     What social joys are there,
   What radiancy of glory,
     What light beyond compare.

2. They stand, those halls of Zion,
     All jubilant with song,
   And bright with many an angel,
     And all the martyr throng;

The Prince is ever in them,
 The daylight is serene;
The pastures of the blessed
 Are deck'd in glorious sheen.

3. There is the throne of David;
 And there, from care released,
The song of them that triumph,
 The shout of them that feast:
And they, who with their Leader,
 Have conquer'd in their fight,
For ever and for ever
 Are clad in robes of white.

29   L. M.

1. There is a fountain filled with blood,
 Drawn from Immanuel's veins;
And sinners, plunged beneath that flood,
 Lose all their guilty stains.

2. The dying thief rejoiced to see
 That fountain in his day;
And there may I, as vile as he,
 Wash all my sins away.

3. Dear, dying Lamb, Thy precious blood
 Shall never lose its power
Till all the ransomed church of God
 Be saved, to sin no more.

4. E'er since, by faith. I saw the stream
 Thy flowing wounds supply,
Redeeming love has been my theme,
 And shall be, till I die.

5. Then in a nobler, sweeter song,
 I'll sing Thy power to save,
When this poor, lisping, stam'ring tongue,
 Lies silent in the grave.

30   S. M.

1. Not all the blood of beasts,
     On Jewish altars slain,
   Could give the guilty conscience peace,
     Or wash away the stain.

2. But Christ, the heavenly Lamb,
     Takes all our sins away:
   A sacrifice of nobler name,
     And richer blood than they.

3. My faith would lay her hand
     On that dear head of Thine,
   While as a penitent I stand,
     And there confess my sin.

4. Believing, we rejoice,
     To see the curse remove;
   We bless the Lamb with cheerful voice,
     And sing His bleeding love.

31   8s & 7s.

1. Love divine, all love excelling,
     Joy of heaven, to earth come down!
   Fix in us Thy humble dwelling,
     All Thy faithful mercies crown.
   Jesus, Thou art all compassion,
     Pure, unbounded love Thou art;
   Visit us with Thy salvation,
     Enter every trembling heart!

2. Breathe, oh, breathe Thy lovely spirit
     Into every troubled breast!
   Let us all in Thee inherit,
     Let us find Thy promised rest.
   Take away the love of sinning,
     Alpha and Omega be:
   End of faith, as its beginning,
     Set our hearts at liberty.

3. Come, almighty to deliver,
      Let us all Thy life receive;
   Graciously return, and never,
      Never more Thy temples leave!
   Thee we would be always blessing,
      Serve Thee as Thy hosts above;
   Pray, and praise Thee without ceasing,
      Glory in Thy precious love.

4. Finish then Thy new creation,
      Pure, unspotted may we be;
   Let us see Thy great salvation
      Perfectly restored in Thee!
   Change from glory into glory,
      Till in heaven we take our place,
   Till we cast our crowns before Thee,
      Lost in wonder, love, and praise.

32   C. M.

1. How sweet the name of Jesus sounds
      In a believer's ear!
   It soothes his sorrows, heals his wounds,
      And drives away his fear.

2. It makes the wounded spirit whole,
      And calms the troubled breast;
   'Tis manna to the hungry soul,
      And to the weary, rest.

3. Weak is the effort of my heart,
      And cold my warmest thought;
   But when I see Thee as Thou art,
      I'll praise Thee as I ought.

4. Till then I would Thy love proclaim,
      With every fleeting breath;
   And may the music of Thy name
      Refresh my soul in death.

33   7s.

1. Children of the heavenly King,
      As ye journey, sweetly sing;

Sing your Saviour's worthy praise,
Glorious in His works and ways.

2. Ye are traveling home to God,
   In the way the fathers trod;
   They are happy now, and ye
   Soon their happiness shall see.

3. Shout, ye little flock, and blest;
   You on Jesus' throne shall rest:—
   There your seat is now prepared,
   There your kingdom and reward.

4. Lord, submissive make us go,
   Gladly leaving all below;
   Only Thou our leader be,
   And we still will follow Thee.

34   L. M.

1. I was a wandering sheep,
     I did not love the fold;
   I did not love my Shepherd's voice,
     I would not be controlled:
   I was a wayward child,
     I did not love my home,
   I did not love my Father's voice,
     I loved afar to roam.

2. The Shepherd sought His sheep,
     The Father sought His child;
   They followed me o'er vale and hill,
     O'er deserts waste and wild:
   They found me nigh to death,
     Famish'd, and faint, and lone;
   They bound me with the bands of love,
     They saved the wandering one.

3. Jesus my Shepherd is,
     'Twas He that loved my soul,
   'Twas He that washed me in His blood,
     'Twas He that made me whole:

'Twas He that sought the lost,
   That found the wanderingsheep,
'Twas He that brought me to the fold—
   'Tis He that still doth keep.

4. No more a wand'ring sheep,
      I love to be controll'd,
   I love my tender Shepherd's voice,
      I love the peaceful fold:
   No more a wayward child,
      I seek no more to roam,
   I love my heavenly Father's voice—
      I love, I love His home.

35 S. M.

1. A charge to keep I have,
      A God to glorify;
   A never-dying soul to save,
      And fit it for the sky.

2. To serve the present age,
      My calling to fulfill;
   Oh, may it all my powers engage
      To do my Master's will.

3. Arm me with jealous care,
      As in Thy sight to live;
   And oh! Thy servant, Lord, prepare,
      A strict account to give.

4. Help me to watch and pray
      And on Thyself rely,
   Assured, if I my trust betray,
      I shall forever die.

36 P. M.

1. A mighty Stronghold is our God,
      A sure defence and weapon;
   He helps us free from every need
      Which hath us now o'ertaken.
         The old angry foe

Now means us deadly woe;
Deep guile and great might
Are His dread arms in fight,—
On earth is not his equal.

2. In our own strength can nought be done—
Our loss were soon effected;
There fights for us the Proper One,
By God Himself elected.
Ask you who frees us?
It is Christ Jesus—
The Lord Sabaoth,
There is no other God;
He'll hold the field of battle.

3. And were the world with devils filled,
All waiting to devour us;
We'll still succeed, so God hath willed,—
They cannot overpower us:
The Prince of this world
To hell shall be hurled;
He seeks to alarm,
But shall do us no harm;
The smallest Word can fell him.

4. The Word they still must let remain,
And for that have no merit;
For He is with us on the plain,
By His good gifts and Spirit;
Destroy they our life,
Goods, fame, child and wife?
Let all pass amain,
They still no conquest gain,
For ours is still the kingdom.

37 S. M.

1. One sweetly solemn thought
Comes to me o'er and o'er:
I'm nearer to my home to-day
Than e'er I've been before;

2. Nearer my Father's house,
   Where many mansions be,
   Nearer the throne where Jesus reigns,
   Nearer the crystal sea.

3. Nearer the bound of life
   Where burdens are laid down,
   Nearer leaving the cross of grief,
   Nearer gaining the crown.

4. But lying dark between,
   And winding through the night,
   Flows on the deep and unknown stream,
   That leads me to the light.

5. Jesus, perfect my trust,
   Strengthen my hand of faith,
   And be Thou near me when I stand
   Upon the shore of death.

38   L. M.

1. Just as I am, without one plea.
   But that Thy Blood was shed for me,
   And that Thou bidd'st me come to Thee,
   O Lamb of God, I come!

2. Just as I am, and waiting not
   To rid my soul of one dark blot,
   To Thee whose Blood can cleanse each
           spot,
   O Lamb of God, I come!

3. Just as I am, though tossed about
   With many a conflict, many a doubt,
   Fightings and fears, within, without,
   O Lamb of God, I come!

4. Just as I am, poor, wretched, blind,
   Sight. healing, riches of the mind,
   Yea. all I need, in Thee to find,
   O Lamb of God, I come!

MISSIONS.

39 L. M.

1. Jesus shall reign where'er the sun
Does his successive journeys run;
His kingdom stretch from shore to shore,
Till moons shall wax and wane no more.

2. People and realms of ev'ry tongue
Dwell on His love with grateful song;
And with united hearts proclaim
That grace and truth by Jesus came.

3. Blessings abound where'er He reigns:
The pris'ner leaps to loose his chains,
The weary find eternal rest,
And all the sons of want are blest.

4. Where He displays His healing power,
The sting of death is known no more:
In Him the sons of Adam boast
More blessings than their father lost.

40 7s & 6s.

1. From Greenland's icy mountains,
From India's coral strand,
Where Afric's sunny fountains
Roll down their golden sand—
From many an ancient river,
From many a palmy plain,
They call us to deliver
Their land from error's chain.

2. What though the spicy breezes
Blow soft o'er Ceylon's Isle;
Though ev'ry prospect pleases,
And only man is vile;
In vain with lavish kindness
The gifts of God are strewn;
The heathen, in his blindness,
Bows down to wood and stone!

3. Shall we, whose souls are lighted
   With wisdom from on high—
Shall we, to men benighted,
   The lamp of life deny ?
Salvation, oh, salvation!
   The joyful sound proclaim,
Till earth's remotest nation
   Has learned Messiah's name.

4. Waft, waft, ye winds, His story,
   And you, ye waters, roll,
Till, like a sea of glory,
   It spreads from pole to pole;
Till o'er our ransom'd nature
   The Lamb for sinners slain,
Redeemer, King, Creator,
   In bliss returns to reign!

41   C. M.

1. Lord, send Thy word, and let it fly
   Arm'd with Thy Spirit's power;
Ten thousand shall confess its sway,
   And bless the saving hour.

2. Beneath the influence of Thy grace,
   The barren wastes shall rise,
With verdure and with fruits array'd,
   A blooming paradise.

3. True holiness shall strike its root
   In each regen'rate heart;
Shall in a growth divine arise,
   And heavenly fruits impart.

4. Lord, for those days we wait—those days
   Are in Thy word foretold;
Fly swifter, sun and stars, and bring
   This promised age of gold.

42   7s.

1. Hasten, Lord, the glorious time,
   When, beneath Messiah's sway,

Ev'ry nation, ev'ry clime,
Shall the Gospel call obey.

2. Mightiest kings His power shall own,
Heathen tribes His name adore;
Satan and his host, o'erthrown,
Bound in chains, shall hurt no more.

3. Then shall war and tumult cease,
Then be banished grief and pain;
Righteousness and joy and peace
Undisturb'd shall ever reign.

4. Bless we, then, our gracious Lord,
Ever praise His glorious name;
All His mighty acts record,
All His wondrous love proclaim.

43   L. M.

1. O Spirit of the living God,
In all Thy plentitude of grace,
Wher'er the foot of man hath trod,
Descend on our apostate race.

2. Be darkness, at Thy coming, light,
Confusion, order, in Thy path:
Souls without strength inspire with might:
Bid mercy triumph over wrath.

3. Baptize the nations far and nigh,
The triumphs of the Cross record;
The name of Jesus glorify,
Till ev'ry kindred call Him Lord.

44   L. M.

1. The heathen perish day by day,
Thousands on thousands pass away;
O Christians, to their rescue fly,
Preach Jesus to them ere they die.

2. Wealth, labor, talents, freely give,
Yea, life itself, that they may live.
What hath your Saviour done for you?
And what for Him will ye not do?

3. Thou Spirit of the Lord, go forth;
Call in the south, awake the north;
Of every clime, from sun to sun,
Gather God's children into one.

45*   H. M.

1. O'er hoarse Atlantic's wave,
From Afric comes the cry,
O Christians! haste and save,
Ere in our want we die!
Our starving souls have ne'er been fed;
Oh! bring to us the Living Bread!

2. And broad Pacific's shore
Re-echoes with the call,
From China wafted o'er,
Beseeching one and all
To kindle in the Flowery clime
The Lamp of Life, the Light divine.

3. And India's myriad sons
Stretch forth their dusky hands;
Crying, O favored ones
Who dwell in Gospel lands,
Send to our longing, thirsty souls
The stream that with salvation rolls.

4. And shall we careless live
With these great gifts in store?
Nor from our fullness give
To spread from shore to shore
Glad tidings from the courts above
Of our Immanuel's boundless love?

5. Pardon our coldness, Lord!
Our languid souls inspire.
May Thy life-giving Word
Kindle a holy fire
In every heart that owns Thy sway,
And hasten the Millenial day!

---

* Written by Miriam.

46 8s, 7s.

1. Go, tell the nations Christ is King,
   His hands the world uphold,
He guides each planet's shining ring,
   And spreads the cloud's dark fold,
Go, cast the false gods in the dust,
   The idols trample down,
   And place in Him your only trust,
For Jesus wears the crown.

2. Go, tell the nations of the blood
   On Calv'ry freely spilt,
The healing streams, the precious flood,
   To wash away their guilt.
Tell them to trust no human rites,
   That earthly gold is dross;
And yet to pardon God delights,
   Since Jesus bore the cross.

3. Go, tell the nations of the hope,
   The joy by Jesus giv'n,
And bid the darkened eyes look up,
   Beyond the stars, to heav'n.
Oh, let your hearts with love o'erflow
   'Cross o'er the heaving tide,
Till all the lands of earth shall know
   The Crowned, once Crucified.

47 8s, 7s.

1. Lord, her watch Thy Church is keeping,
   When shall earth Thy rule obey?
When shall end the night of weeping,
   When shall break the promised day?
See the whitening harvest languish,
   Waiting still the laborer's toil.
Was in vain Thy Son's deep anguish,
   Shall the strong retain the spoil?

2. Tidings send to every creature—
   Millions yet have never heard;

Can they hear without a preacher?
  Lord Almighty, give the Word!
Give the Word! in every nation,
  Let the Gospel trumpet sound,
Witnessing a world's salvation,
  To the earth's remotest bound.

3. Then the end! Thy Church completed,
  All Thy chosen gathered in.
With their King in glory seated,
  Satan bound, and banished sin;
Gone forever, parting, weeping,
  Hunger, sorrow, death, and pain.
Lo! her watch Thy Church is keeping.
  Come, Lord Jesus, come to reign.

48   7s, 6s.

1. The watchers on the mountain
  Proclaim the Bridegroom nigh;
Go, meet Him as He cometh,
  And glad hosannas cry!
Around the throne of glory,
  The Lamb ye shall behold;
In triumph, cast before Him
  Your diadems of gold!

2. Rejoice ye, then, believing,
  And let your lights appear;
Though evening is advancing,
  And darker night is near,
The Bridegroom is arising,
  And soon He draweth nigh;
Up, pray, and watch, and wrestle,—
  At midnight comes the cry!

3 Our Hope and Expectation,
  O Jesus, now appear:
Arise, thou Sun, so longed for,
  And banish every fear:
With hearts and hands uplifted,

We plead, O Lord, to see
The day of our redemption,
That brings us unto Thee!

49   7s.

1. Watchman! tell us of the night,
   What its signs of promise are.
   Trav'ler! o'er yon mountain's height
   See the glory-beaming star!
   Watchman! does its beauteous ray
   Aught of joy or hope foretell!
   Trav'ler! yes; it brings the day,
   Promised day of Israel.

2. Watchman! tell us of the night:
   Higher yet that star ascends.
   Trav'ler! blessedness and light,
   Peace and truth its course portends.
   Watchman! will its beams alone
   Gild the spot that gave them birth?
   Trav'ler! ages are its own;
   See! it bursts o'er all the earth!

3. Watchman! tell us of the night,
   For the morning seems to dawn.
   Trav'ler! darkness takes its flight;
   Doubt and terror are withdrawn.
   Watchman! let thy wand'rings cease;
   Hie thee to thy quiet home.
   Trav'ler! lo! the Prince of Peace,
   Lo! the Son of God is come!

50   L. M.

1. Ye Christian heralds, go, proclaim
   Salvation in Immanuel's name;
   To distant climes the tidings bear,
   And plant the rose of Sharon there.

2. He'll shield you with a wall of fire,
   With flaming zeal your breasts inspire,

Bid raging winds their fury cease,
And calm the savage breast to peace.

3. And when our labors all are o'er,
Then we shall meet to part no more;
Meet with the blood-bought throng to fall,
And crown our Jesus, Lord of all.

51*   6s, 4s.

1. O man of God, arise!
A voice sounds from the skies;
Awake, 'tis day!
Behold the fields in sight,
The harvest glows with light;
Put in your sickle bright;
Up and away!

2. My work is great—be strong;
The day of toil is long;
Seek help divine.
The dangers may appall—
Thy heart within thee fall—
Upon Me always call;
My strength is thine.

3. My love has tinged the cross,
Your soul to save from loss,
In endless night.
Let love reign in thy heart,
My truth and zeal impart;
Thus to the fields depart,
With holy might.

4. The reaper shall be blest,
The toiler have his rest,
My word I give.
Like Me thou shalt appear,
From sin forever clear;
Secure from ev'ry fear,
With Me to live.

* Written by Rev. H. K. Fenner.

52   7s, 6s.

1. There comes a wail of an anguish
     Across the ocean wave:
   It pleads for help, O Christians,
     Poor, dying souls to save.
   Those far-off heathen nations
     Who sit in darkest night,
   Now stretch their hands imploring,
     And cry to us for light.

2. We have the blessed Gospel,
     We know its priceless worth:
   We read the grand old story
     Of Christ, the Saviour's, birth.
   O haste, ye faithful workers!
     To them the tidings bear,
   Glad tidings of salvation,
     That they our light may share.

3. Go, plant the cross of Jesus
     On each benighted shore,
   Go, wave the Gospel banner
     Till darkness reigns no more;
   And while the seed you scatter,
     Far o'er the ocean's foam,
   We'll pray for you and labor
     In mission fields at home.

53   10s.

1. Over the ocean wave, far, far away,
   There the poor heathen live, waiting for day;
   Groping in ignorance, dark as the night,
   No blessed Bible to give them the light.

CHORUS.

Pity them, pity them, Christians at home,
Haste with the bread of life, hasten and come.

2. Here in this happy land, we have the light,
   Shining from God's own Word, free, pure
       and bright;

Shall we not send to them Bibles to read,
Teachers and preachers, and all that they
    need?—CHO.

3. Then, while the mission ships glad tidings
        bring,
    List! as that heathen band joyfully sing,
    "Over the ocean wave, oh, see them come,
    Bringing the bread of life, guiding us home."
    —CHO.

54*

1. The sun is sinking o'er the mountains far,
    To Shine in lands that lie beyond our
        sight—
    Thine own, Oh, Father! all earth's na-
        tions are:—
    O give to them the Light.

2. Earth hath no shadow like Thy veiled face,
    No sunshine like the knowledge that
        Thou art.
    Shine forth, great Light! in every dark-
        en'd place:—
    Make glad each weary heart.

3. Shine in Thy messengers who bear Thy
        light,
    From home and dear ones though they
        dwell afar:
    Since Thou art with them, may they know
        no night.
    Be Thou their guiding star.

4. And when heaven's morning dawneth for
        us all,
    With earthly sun and shade forever
        past,
    From every land Thou wilt Thy children
        call,
    To dwell in light at last.

---

* Written by Laura Wade Rice.

55   7s, 6s.

1. The morning light is breaking.
   The darkness disappears:
   The sons of earth are waking
   To penitential tears.
   Each breeze that sweeps the ocean
   Brings tidings from afar
   Of nations in commotion,
   Prepared for Zion's war.

2. See heathen nations bending
   Before the God we love,
   And thousand hearts ascending
   In gratitude above:
   While sinners, now confessing,
   The Gospel call obey,
   And seek the Saviour's blessing—
   A nation in a day.

3. Blest river of salvation,
   Pursue thine onward way;
   Flow thou to every nation,
   Nor in thy richness stay:
   Stay not till all the lowly
   Triumphant reach their home;
   Stay not till all the holy
   Proclaim—"The Lord is come."

56   7s, 6s.

1. When shall the voice of singing
   Flow joyfully along?
   When hill and valley ringing
   With one triumphant song,
   Proclaim the contest ended,
   And Him who once was slain
   Again to earth descended
   In righteousness to reign.

2. Then from the craggy mountains
   The sacred shout shall fly,

And shady vales and fountains
  Shall echo the reply:
High tower and lowly dwelling
  Shall send the chorus round,
The hallelujah swelling
  In one eternal sound.

57   C. M.

1. Pity the nations, O our God!
     Constrain the earth to come;
   Send Thy victorious word abroad,
     And bring the strangers home.

2. We long to see Thy churches full,
     That all Thy faithful race
   May, with one voice and heart and soul,
     Sing Thy redeeming grace.

58*   8s, 7s., Double.

1. Hosts of God go forth to battle
     In His name and for His laws:
   Wrong and sin are camped around you,
     Onward! 'tis a glorious cause.
   Christ is such a mighty Leader—
     Though the fight be hard and long,
   That the end is surely victory,
     Heaven will shout the conqueror's song.

2. Bound in chains your brethren languish,
     Slaved by Satan, kept by sin:
   Force a way to darkest dungeons,
     Let the glorious Light stream in.
   Only Jesus can release them,
     He, your Captain, points the way;
   Follow, follow. He is waiting:
     Where He leads should we delay?

3. Dare we rest in ease and pleasure,
     Call our lives or gold our own,
   While, in heathen darkness lying,

Written by Laura Wade Rice.

Millions bow to gods of stone?
Beds of ease are Satan's dungeons,
  Liberty *with Christ* is found,
And His hosts are ever marching
  Onward to new battle-ground.

3. Forward, then, ye ransomed captives!
  Christ, the Leader, set you free!
Since He saved you from the dungeon,
  March with Him to victory!
Living for Him, dying for Him,
  Noblest souls were ever found
With this Leader and such comrades—
  This is glorious battle-ground.

59   L. M.

1. Eternal Father, Thou hast said,
  That Christ all glory shall obtain;
That He who once a sufferer bled
  Shall o'er the world a conqu'ror reign.

2. We wait Thy triumph, Saviour King;
  Long ages have prepared Thy way;
Now all abroad Thy banner fling—
  Set time's great battle in array.

3. Thy hosts are mustered to the field;
  "The Cross!" the Cross!" the battle
    call;
The old grim tow'rs of darkness yield,
  And soon shall totter to their fall.

4. On mountain tops the watch-fires glow,
  Where scattered wide the watchmen
    stand;
Voice echoes voice, and onward flow
  The joyous shouts from land to land.

60   C. M., Double.

1. The Son of God goes forth to war,
  A kingly crown to gain:
His blood-red banner streams afar.

Who follows in His train?
Who best can drink his cup of woe,
Triumphant over pain:
Who patient bears his cross below—
He follows in His train.

2. The martyr first, whose eagle eye
Could pierce beyond the grave,
Who saw his Master in the sky
And called on Him to save;
Like Him, with pardon on His tongue
In midst of mortal pain,
He prayed for them that did the wrong—
Who follows in His train?

3. A glorious band, the chosen few,
On whom the Spirit came:
Twelve valiant saints, their hope they
knew,
And mocked the cross and shame:
They met the tyrant's brandished steel,
The lion's gory mane:
They bowed their necks, the death to feel—
Who follows in their train?

61*   7s, 6s.

1. Great Captain of Salvation,
Lift up Thy standard high,
Thy Truth reach ev'ry nation
Beneath the bending sky:
Where'er the night rejoices:
With kindling star on star;
There let the Gospel voices,
Go forth to realms afar.

2. Where'er earth's gladsome waters
Go flashing to the sea,
There let her sons and daughters
Thy willing subjects be;

---

* By permission of Rev. J. E. Rankin, D. D., Washington, D. C.

Where'er the circling ocean
  Kisses the peopled shore,
Let men pay their devotion,
  And Thee as God adore.

3. Great Captain of Salvation,
  Send Thy last mandates forth:
O South, go take thy station,
  And keep not back, O North;
Soon may the note victorious
  Break forth like sea on sea,
And Thy fair legions glorious
  Win this lost world to Thee!

62*

1. Read o'er your marching orders,
  Sealed with your Leader's blood;
To earth's remotest borders
  Proclaim the Lamb of God!
Set life and death before them,
  The Jew as well as Greek;
One God and Father o'er them,
  That Father bid them seek.

2 Read o'er your marching orders!
  Who knows as well as He
The depth of sin's disorders,
  Its curse and misery?
In Christ there is salvation
  From sin and death and hell;
To every tribe and nation
  Let the sweet tidings swell.

3. Waste not on speculation
  The force for toil you need;
To all the great salvation
  On wings of angels speed:
Swerve not to realms forbidden,

---

* By permission of Rev. J. E. Rankin, D. D., Washington, D. C.

Where no man's feet have trod;
Some things God's love has hidden,
Sôme things belong to God.

4 Enough for you the mission,
   The Gospel tale to tell;
This is the great commission
   To all on earth that dwell.
Read o'er your marching orders;
   His flag must be unfurled
In earth's remotest borders,
   Must float all round the world.

63   7s, 6s.

1. Lift high the royal standard,
   For Christ has saved from sin;
Upon the cross He suffered
   To bring Salvation in;
Go tell the heathen nations,
   Who in their sorrows dwell,
That Christ, the Prince of Glory,
   Redeems from death and hell.

2. Filled with the love of Jesus,
   Our prayers like incense rise;
And Christ, our royal Captain,
   Is smiling from the skies.
The ark of God is moving,
   The heathen temples fall;
We'll take the world for Jesus,
   And crown Him Lord of all.

64   6s, 5s

1. Bear the message onward!
   Spread it far and wide;
Let the distant nations
   Know that Jesus died;
Died, that God might justly
   Sinners now forgive;
Died, that through His merit,
   Guilty man might live.

CHORUS.

Bear the message onward!
  Spread it far and wide;
Let the distant nations
  Know that Jesus died.

2. Bear the message onward!
     Over land and sea:
  Nothing, save the Gospel,
     Makes men noble,—free.
  Spread, O spread the teaching
     Fraught with endless bliss;
  Angels well might covet
     Work so grand as this.—CHO.

3. Bear the message onward!
     'Tis so grandly true;
  Wheresoe'er it cometh
     Eden blooms anew.
  Work performed for Jesus
     Cannot go unblessed;
  Not till life is ended
     Must God's servants rest.—CHO.

65   8s, 7s.

1. Come, Thou long expected Jesus,
     Born to set Thy people free;
  From our fears and sins release us;
     Let us find our rest in Thee.

2. Israel's Strength and Consolation,
     Hope of all the earth, Thou art,
  Dear Desire of every nation,
     Joy of every longing heart.

3. Born Thy people to deliver;
     Born a Child, and yet a King;
  Born to reign o'er us forever,
     Now Thy gracious kingdom bring.

4. By Thine own eternal Spirit
   Rule in all our hearts alone;
   By Thine all-sufficient merit
   Raise us to Thy glorious throne.

66   L. M.

1. Behold th' expected time draw near,
   The shades disperse, the dawn appear,
   The barren wilderness assume
   The beauteous tints of Eden's bloom.

2. Events with prophecies conspire
   To raise our faith, our zeal to fire;
   The rip'ning fields, already white,
   Present a harvest to our sight.

3. Come, let us with a grateful heart
   In this blest labor share a part;
   Our prayers and off'rings gladly bring
   To aid the triumphs of our King.

67   S. M.

1. Come, Lord, and tarry not;
   Bring the long looked-for day;
   Oh, why these years of waiting here,
   These ages of delay.

2. Come, for Thy saints still wait;
   Daily ascends their sigh;
   The Spirit and the Bride say, Come,
   Dost Thou not hear the cry?

3. Come, and make all things new;
   Build up this ruined earth;
   Restore our faded Paradise,
   Creation's second birth.

4. Come, and begin Thy reign
   Of everlasting peace;
   Come, take the kingdom to Thyself,
   Great King of righteousness.

68 8s, 7s., Double.

1. Saviour, sprinkle many nations,
    Fruitful let Thy sorrows be;
By Thy pains and consolations,
    Draw the Gentiles unto Thee.
Of Thy cross, the wondrous story,
    Be it to the nations told;
Let them see Thee in Thy glory,
    And Thy mercy manifold.

2. Far and wide, though all unknowing,
    Pants for Thee each mortal breast;
Human tears for Thee are flowing,
    Human hearts in Thee would rest,
Thirsting, as for dews of even,
    As the new-mown grass for rain;
Thee they seek, as God of Heaven,
    Thee, as Man, for sinners slain.

3. Saviour, lo! the isles are waiting,
    Stretch'd the hand, and strain'd the
        sight,
For Thy Spirit, new creating,
    Love's pure flame and wisdom's light.
Give the word, and of the preacher
    Speed the foot and touch the tongue,
Till on earth by ev'ry creature
    Glory to the Lamb be sung.

69 8s, 7s., Double.

1. Glorious things of thee are spoken,
    Zion, city of our God:
He, whose word cannot be broken,
    Form'd thee for His own abode:
On the Rock of Ages founded,
    What can shake thy sure repose?
With salvation's walls surrounded,
    Thou may'st smile at all thy foes.

2. See the streams of living waters,
    Springing from eternal love,
  Well supply thy sons and daughters,
    And all fear of want remove:
  Who can faint while such a river
    Ever flows, thy thirst t' assauge?
  Grace which, like the Lord, the Giver,
    Never fails from age to age.

3. Round each habitation hov'ring,
    See the cloud and fire appear!
  For a glory and a cov'ring,
    Showing that the Lord is near:
  Thus deriving from their banner
    Light by night and shade by day;
  Safe they feed upon the manna
    Which He gives them when they pray.

70   7s, 6 lines.

1. On Thy Church, O Power divine,
  Cause Thy glorious face to shine,
  Till the nations from afar
  Hail her as their guiding star;
  Till her sons, from zone to zone,
  Make Thy great salvation known;

2. Then shall God, with lavish hand,
  Scatter blessings o'er the land;
  Earth shall yield her rich increase,
  Every breeze shall whisper peace,
  And the world's remotest bound
  With the voice of praise resound.

71   S. M.

1. O Lord, our God! arise:
    The cause of truth maintain,
  And wide all o'er the peopled world
    Extend her blessed reign.

2. Thou Prince of Life! arise,
    Nor let Thy glory cease;

Far spread the conquests of Thy grace,
And bless the earth with peace.

3. O Holy Spirit! rise,
Expand Thy heavenly wing,
And o'er a dark and ruin'd world
Let light and order spring.

4. Oh, all ye nations! rise,
To God the Saviour sing;
From shore to shore, from earth to heaven,
Let echoing anthems ring.

72   S. M.

1. I love Thy Zion, Lord,
The house of Thine abode,
The Church, O blest Redeemer, saved
By Thine own precious blood.

2. I love Thy Church, O God,
Her walls before Thee stand,
Dear as the apple of Thine eye,
And graven on Thy hand.

3. If e'er to bless Thy sons
My voice or hands deny,
These hands let useful skill forsake,
This voice in silence die.

4. Beyond my highest joy
I prize her heavenly ways,
Her sweet communion, solemn vows,
Her hymns of love and praise.

73   7s, 6s.

1. The Church's one foundation
Is Jesus Christ, her Lord;
She is His new creation
By water and the Word:
From heaven He came and sought her,
To be His holy Bride;
With His own blood He bought her,
And for her life He died.

2. 'Mid toil and tribulation,
    And tumult of her war,
  She 'waits the consummation
    Of peace for evermore;
  Till with the vision glorious
    Her longing eyes are blest,
  And the great Church victorious
    Shall be the Church at rest.

3. Yet she on earth hath union
    With God, the Three in One,   .
  And mystic, sweet communion
    With those whose rest is won.
  O happy ones, and holy!
    Lord, give us grace, that we
  Like them, the meek and lowly,
    On high, may dwell with Thee.

74

1. Christ, the Lord, is ris'n again,
    Hallelujah!
  Christ hath broken ev'ry chain:
    Hallelujah!
  Hark! angelic voices cry,
    Hallelujah!
  Singing evermore on high,
    Hallelujah!

2. He, who slumber'd in the grave,
    Hallelujah!
  Is exalted now to save:
    Hallelujah!
  Now thro' Christendom it rings,
    Hallelujah!
  That the Lamb is King of kings:
    Hallelujah!

3. Now He bids us tell abroad,
    Hallelujah!
  How the lost may be restored,
    Hallelujah!

How the penitent forgiv'n,
    Hallelujah!
How we, too, may enter heav'n:
    Hallelujah!

4. Thou, our Paschal Lamb indeed,
    Hallelujah!
Christ, Thy ransomed people feed!
    Hallelujah!
Take our sins and guilt away,
    Hallelujah!
That we all may sing for aye,
    Hallelujah!

75   7s

1. Wake the song of jubilee!
Let it echo o'er the sea:
Now is come the promised hour:
Jesus reigns with sov'reign power.

2. All ye nations, join and sing,
"Christ, of lords and kings, is King!"
Let it sound from shore to shore,
"Jesus reigns for evermore!"

3. Now the desert lands rejoice,
And the islands join their voice;
Joy! the whole creation sings,
"Jesus is the King of kings!"

76   7s, 6s.

1. Hail to the Lord's Annointed,
    Great David's greater Son!
Hail, in the time appointed,
    His reign on earth begun!
He comes to break oppression,
    To set the captive free,
To take away transgression,
    And rule in equity.

2. He comes with succor speedy,
    To those who suffer wrong;

To help the poor and needy,
  And bid the weak be strong;
To give them songs for sighing,
  Their darkness turn to light,
Whose souls, condemn'd and dying,
  Were precious in His sight.

3. He shall descend like showers
  Upon the fruitful earth,
And love and joy, like flowers,
  Spring in His path to birth;
Before Him, on the mountains,
  Shall peace the herald, go:
And righteousness, in fountains,
  From hill to valley flow.

4. For Him shall prayer unceasing,
  And daily vows ascend,
His kingdom still increasing,
  A kingdom without end:
The tide of time shall never
  His covenant remove;
His name shall stand for ever;
  That name to us is love.

7s.

1. Hark! the song of jubilee,
  Loud as mighty thunders roar,
Or the fullness of the sea
  When it breaks upon the shore:
Hallelujah! for the Lord
  God Omnipotent shall reign;
Hallelujah! let the word
  Echo round the earth and main!

2. Hallelujah! hark the sound,
  From the depth unto the skies,
Wakes above, beneath, around,
  All creation's harmonies:
See Jehovah's banner furled,

Sheath'd His sword, He speaks, 'tis done:
And the kingdoms of this world
Are the kingdoms of His Son.

3. He shall reign from pole to pole
With illimitable sway;
He shall reign when, like a scroll,
Yonder heavens have pass'd away:
Then the end—beneath His rod
Man's last enemy shall fall;
Hallelujah! Christ is God,
God in Christ is all in all.

HOME MISSIONS.

78* 6s, 4s.

1. Here, in this glorious land,
Firmly we take our stand,
O Son of God!
Battling right valiantly,
Till hosts of evil flee—
Grant us the victory,
Strong Son of God!

2. Here, where our fathers came,
Seeking, in Thy great Name,
Blest Son of God!
Freedom to worship Thee,
O, may all men be free
From sin's vile slavery,
Pure Son of God!

3. Founded in love and praise,
Strong Son of God!
Kept by a chosen band,
Sworn to obey command,
Led by Thine own right hand,
Great Son of God!

* Written by Laura Wade Rice.

4. And if our lives we give,
Dying, that men may live,
    Dear Son of God!
Heaven's gates will open wide,
And at the Conqueror's side
Will we for aye abide,
    Crown'd Son of God!

79   6s, 4s.

1. God bless our native land!
Firm may she ever stand,
    Through storm and night;
When the wild tempests rave,
Ruler of wind and wave,
Do Thou our country save
    By Thy great might.

2. For her our prayer shall rise
To God, above the skies;
    On Him we wait:
Thou, who art ever nigh,
Guarding with watchful eye,
To Thee aloud we cry,
    God save the State!

80*

1. From Western prairies calling,
    The cry comes strong and clear:
"Our brothers now are falling,
    O, send the Gospel near;"
Tell out the gladsome tidings
    Of Christ our Saviour's birth;
The Holy Spirit's guidings
    Proclaim through all the earth.

2. Forgot not those now parted
    Far from their friends of youth,
Who, in the way once started,

* Written by Nina Charles Schnur.

Have now forgot the truth.
O, tell them Christ receiveth
All such who humbly say,
"O Lord, Thy child believeth,
Though now gone far astray."

3. So thus the story telling,
From East to West repeat,
Till high the chorus swelling
Shall reach the mercy-seat:
"Columbia is Thy nation:
Our land for Christ is won:
Soon shall the whole creation
Bow down before Thy throne."

81*

1. Father, Thou who hearest pleading,
When in faith Thy children pray;
Look upon our land in mercy;
Speed, oh, speed the glorious day
When to Jesus,
Every heart shall tribute pay.

2. Where, like emerald seas, the prairies
Roll their flower-sprayed waves around,
Let us launch the good ship Zion,
Make the Word of God abound;
May His praises
To the vaulted skies resound.

3. Where the lofty snow-crowned mountains
Of the wild Sierra's chain
Veil their heads in heaven's azure,
Waft we, too, the glad refrain—
"Jesus loves thee;
Come, a crown of life obtain."

4. Where the tropic sun is glowing;
'Neath the still, cold Northern skies;
Where the fierce Atlantic rages;

---

* Written by Catherine Dentzer.

Where the calm Pacific lies,
  Unto Jesus
From all hearts may prayers arise.

5. May we make our land a Canaan,
  Which shall place of worship be,
Where the children of all nations,
  To one God shall bend the knee.
    Thine the glory,
  Father, Son and Spirit, Three.

82

1. Our country's voice is pleading,
  Ye men of God arise.
His providence is leading,
  The land before you lies;
Day-gleams are o'er it brightening,
  And promise clothes the soil;
Wide fields, for harvest whitening,
  Invite the reaper's toil.

2. Go, where the waves are breaking
  On California's shore,
Christ's precious Gospel taking,
  More rich than golden ore;
On Alleghany's mountains,
  Through all the Western vale,
Beside Missouri's fountains,
  Rehearse the wondrous tale.

3. The love of Christ unfolding,
  Speed on from east to west,
Till all, His cross beholding,
  In Him are fully blest.
Great Author of salvation,
  Haste, haste the glorious day,
When we, a ransomed nation,
  Thy sceptre shall obey.

83   8s, 7s.

1. Hark! the voice of Jesus saying,
  "Who will go and work to-day;

Fields are white and harvests waiting:
  Who will bear the sheaves away?"
Loud and strong the Master calleth,
  Rich rewards He offers thee.
Who will answer, gladly saying,
  "Here am I, send me, send me."

2. If you cannot cross the ocean,
    And the heathen lands explore,
  You can find the heathen nearer,
    You can help them at your door.
  If you cannot give your thousands,
    You can give your widow's mite,
  And the least you do for Jesus
    Will be precious in His sight.

3. Let none hear you idly saying,
    "There is nothing I can do,"
  While the souls of men are dying,
    And the Master calls for you.
  Take the task He gives you gladly,
    Let His work your pleasure be;
  Answer quickly, when He calleth,
    "Here am I, send me, send me."

WORK.

84   7s, 6s.

1. Work, for the night is coming,
    Work thro' the morning hours;
  Work while the dew is sparkling,
    Work 'mid springing flow'rs;
  Work when the day grows brighter,
    Work in the glowing sun.
  Work, for the night is coming,
    When man's work is done.

2. Work, for the night is coming,
    Work thro' the sunny noon;
  Fill brightest hours with labor,

Rest comes sure and soon.
Give ev'ry flying minute
  Something to keep in store;
Work, for the night is coming,
  When man works no more.

3. Work, for the night is coming,
  Under the sunset skies:
While their bright tints are glowing,
  Work, for daylight flies.
Work till the last beam fadeth,
  Fadeth to shine no more;
Work while the night is dark'ning,
  When man's work is o'er.

85   C. M.

1. Am I a soldier of the cross,
  A follower of the Lamb?
And shall I fear to own His cause,
  Or blush to speak His name?

2. Must I be carried to the skies
  On flowery beds of ease?
While others fought to win the prize,
  And sailed through bloody seas.

3. Are there no foes for me to face,
  Must I not stem the flood?
Is this vile world a friend to grace,
  To help me on to God?

4. Sure I must fight, if I would reign;
  Increase my courage, Lord!
I'll bear the toil, endure the pain,
  Supported by Thy Word.

86   L. M.

1. Go, labor on; your hands are weak,
  Your knees are faint, your soul cast
    down,
Yet falter not; the prize you seek
  Is near—a kingdom and a crown!

2 Go, labor on, while it is day;
   The world's dark night is hastening on:
Speed, speed thy work—cast sloth away!
   For thus it is that souls are won.

3. Men die in darkness at your side,
   Without a hope to cheer the tomb:
Take up the torch and wave it wide—
   The torch that lights time's thickest
      gloom.

4. Toil on—faint not—keep watch and pray!
   Be wise the erring soul to win;
Go forth into the world's highway:
   Compel the wanderer to come in.

87   S. M.

1. We give Thee but Thine own,
   Whate'er the gift may be,
For all we have is Thine alone,
   A trust, O Lord, from Thee.

2. To comfort and to bless,
   To find a balm for woe,
To tend the lone and fatherless,
   Is angel's work below.

3. The captive to release,
   To God the lost to bring,
To teach the way of life and peace,
   It is a Christ-like thing.

4. And we believe Thy word,
   Tho' dim our faith may be:
Whate'er for Thine we do, O Lord,
   We do it unto Thee.

88

1. Sowing in the morning, sowing seeds of kind-
      ness,
   Sowing in the noontide and the dewy eves;

Waiting for the harvest, and the time of
    reaping,
We shall come rejoicing, bringing in the
    sheaves.
CHORUS.
Bringing in the sheaves, &c.

2. Sowing in the sunshine, sowing in the shadows,
    Fearing neither clouds nor winter's chill-
        ing breeze;
By and by the harvest, and the labor ended,
    We shall come rejoicing, bringing in the
        sheaves.—CHOR.

3. Go, then, ever weeping, sowing for the Master,
    Tho' the loss sustain'd our spirit often
        grieves;
When our weeping's over, He will bid us
        welcome—
    We shall come rejoicing, bringing in the
        sheaves.—CHOR.

89   8s, 7s.

1. He that goeth forth with weeping,
    Bearing precious seed in love,
Never tiring, never sleeping,
    Findeth mercy from above.

2. Soft descend the dews of heaven,
    Bright the rays celestial, shine;
Precious fruits will thus be given,
    Through an influence all divine.

3. Sow thy seed, be never weary,
    Let no fears thy soul annoy;
Be the prospect e'er so dreary,
    Thou shalt reap the fruits of joy.

4. Lo, the scene of verdure brightening,
    See the rising grain appear!
Look again! the fields are whitening,
    For the harvest time is near.

CHILDREN'S HYMNS.

———✠———

OPENING.

90   H. M.

1. Again we meet, O Lord,
   Again we fill this place,
To hear Thy holy word
   And ask Thy promised grace;
To thank Thee for the gifts we share,
The children of Thy love and care.

2. Grant us the listening ear,
   The understanding heart,
The mind and will sincere,
   To choose the better part—
To take the learner's lowly seat,
And gather wisdom at Thy feet.

3. Through this, and every day,
   Teach us Thy paths to tread;
Nor let our feet astray
   By Satan's wiles be led;
But keep us in the narrrow road,
The way to glory and to God.

91   8s, 7s, 4s.

1. Saviour, like a Shepherd lead us,
   Much we need Thy tend'rest care;
In Thy pleasant pastures feed us,
   For our use Thy folds prepare;
Blessed Jesus, blessed Jesus,
   Thou hast bought us, Thine we are.

2. Thou hast promised to receive us,
   Poor and sinful though we be;
Thou hast mercy to relieve us,

Grace to cleause, and power to free;
Blessed Jesus, blessed Jesus,
Let us early turn to Thee.

3. Early let us seek Thy favor,
Early let us do Thy will;
Blessed Lord and only Saviour,
With Thy love our bosoms fill:
Blessed Jesus, blessed Jesus,
Thou hast loved us, love us still.

92
8s, 7s, 4s.

1. Saviour, at Thy footstool bending,
We, a youthful band, appear;
May our grateful songs ascending,
Reach and please Thy gracious ear;
Thus to praise Thee
Make and keep our hearts sincere.

2. No harsh words of indignation
Drive this little flock from Thee;
Gentle is Thy invitation:
"Suffer them to come to me."
Dearest Saviour,
Let us each Thy kingdom see.

3. Take us, then, Thou kind Protector,
Keep us by Thy watchful care;
Be our Shepherd, Friend, Director;
In Thine arms of mercy bear.
Guide to glory:
We shall dwell in safety there.

93
. 7s, 6s.

1. Dear Saviour, bless the children
Who've gathered here to-day,
O, send Thy Holy Spirit,
And teach us how to pray.

2. Dear Lord, come Thou to help us
Obey Thy great command,

And send the blessed Gospel
Abroad thro' every land.

3. Lord, bless the work we're doing,
  And bless our gifts, though small,
And hear our prayer, for Jesus' sake,
  Who died to save us all.

PRAISE.

94*

1. Praise ye the Father! for His loving kindness,
Tenderly cares He for His erring children;
Praise Him, ye angels, praise Him in the
  heavens,
  Praise ye Jehovah!

2. Praise ye the Saviour! great is His compassion,
Graciously cares He for His chosen people;
Young men and maidens, ye old men and
  children,
  Praise ye the Saviour!

3. Praise ye the Spirit! Comforter of Israel!
Sent of the Father and the Son to bless us;
Praise ye the Father, Son and Holy Spirit,
  Praise ye the Triune God!

95   7s.

1. Glory to the Father give,
  God in whom we move and live;
Children's prayers He deigns to hear,
Children's songs delight His ear.

2. Glory to the Son, we bring,
  Christ, our Prophet, Priest and King;
Children, raise your sweetest strain
To the Lamb, for He was slain.

---

* From Missionary Hymnal, by permission.

3. Glory to the Holy Ghost,
   He reclaims the sinner lost;
   Children's minds may He inspire,
   Touch their tongues with holy fire.

4. Glory in the highest be
   To the blessed Trinity,
   For the Gospel from above,
   For the word that "God is love."

96   8s, 7s.

1. Humble praises, holy Jesus,
   Infant voices raise to Thee;
   In Thy arms, O Lord, receive us,
   Suffer us Thy lambs to be.

2. Blessed Saviour! thou hast bidden
   Babes like us to come to Thee:
   Once by Thy disciples chidden,
   Thou didst bless such ones as we.

3. Thanks to God, who freely gave us
   His beloved Son to die,
   From eternal death to save us:
   Glory be to God on high!

97   7s, 6s.

1. When His salvation bringing,
   To Zion Jesus came,
   The children all stood singing
   Hosanna to His Name;
   Nor did their zeal offend Him,
   But as He rode along,
   He let them still attend Him,
   And smiled to hear their song.

2. And since the Lord retaineth
   His love for children still.
   Though now as King He reigneth
   On Zion's heav'nly hill:
   We'll flock around His banner,

Who sits upon the throne,
And cry aloud "Hosanna
To David's royal Son."

3. For should we fail proclaiming
Our Great Redeemer's praise.
The stones, our silence shaming,
Might well hosanna raise.
But shall we only render
The tribute of our words?
No! while our hearts are tender,
They, too, shall be the Lord's.

98   C. M.

1. Hosanna, be the children's song
To Christ, the children's King;
His praise, to whom their souls belong,
Let all the children sing.

2. Hosanna, sound from hill to hill,
And spread from plain to plain;
While louder, sweeter, clearer still,
Woods echo to the strain.

3. Hosanna, on the wings of light
O'er earth and ocean fly;
Till morn to eve, and noon to night,
And heaven to earth reply.

4. Hosanna, then, our song shall be,
Hosanna to our King;
This is the children's jubilee,
Let all the children sing.

99*

1. Can a little child like me
Thank the Father fittingly?
Yes, oh, yes! be good and true,
Patient, kind, in all you do;

---

* From Spiritual Songs for the Sunday School, by permission.

Love the Lord, and do your part;
Learn to say with all your heart,
    Father, we thank Thee!
    Father, in heaven, we thank Thee!

2. For the fruit upon the tree,
For the birds that sing of Thee,
For the earth in beauty drest,
Father, mother and the rest;
For Thy precious, loving care,
For Thy bounty everywhere,
    Father, we thank Thee!
    Father, in heaven, we thank Thee!

3. For the sunshine warm and bright,
For the day and for the night;
For the lessons of our youth—
Honor, gratitude and truth;
For the love that met us here,
For the home and for the cheer,
    Father, we thank Thee!
    Father, in heaven, we thank Thee!

4. For our comrades and our plays,
And our happy holidays;
For the joyful work, and true,
That a little child may do;
For our lives, but just begun,
For the great gift of Thy Son,
    Father, we thank Thee!
    Father, in heaven, we thank Thee!

100   7s, 6s.

1. Jesus, high in glory,
    Lend a list'ning ear;
When we bow before Thee,
    Children's praises hear.

2. Though Thou art so holy,
    Heaven's Almighty King,
Thou wilt stoop to listen,
    When Thy praise we sing.

3. We are little children,
    Weak and apt to stray;
Saviour, guide and keep us
    In the heavenly way.

4. Save us, Lord, from sinning,
    Watch us day by day;
Help us now to love Thee,
    Take our sins away.

5. Then, when Jesus calls us
    To our heavenly home,
We will gladly answer,
    "Saviour, Lord, we come."

101   7s, 6s.

1. Around the throne of God in heaven,
    Thousands of children stand;
Children whose sins are all forgiven,
    A holy, happy band,
        Singing Glory, Glory, Glory be to
        God on high.

2. In flowing robes of spotless white,
    See every one arrayed;
Dwelling in everlasting light,
    And joys that never fade,
        Singing Glory, Glory, etc.

3. What brought them to that world above,
    That heaven so bright and fair,
Where all is peace and joy and love?
    How came those children there?
        Singing Glory, Glory, etc.

4. Because the Saviour shed His blood
    To wash away their sin;
Bathed in that pure and precious flood,
    Behold them white and clean!
        Singing Glory, Glory, etc.

5. On earth they sought their Saviour's
        grace,
   On earth they loved His Name;
   So now they see His blessed Face,
   And stand before the Lamb,
        Singing Glory, Glory, etc.

102
8s, 5s, 8s, 7s.

1. Angel voices ever singing
        Round Thy throne of light,
   Angel harps forever ringing,
        Rest not day nor night;
   Thousands only live to bless Thee,
        And confess Thee Lord of might.

2. Thou, who art beyond the farthest
        Mental eye can scan,
   Can it be that Thou regardest
        Songs of sinful man?
   Can we feel that thou art near us,
        And wilt hear us? Yea, we can.

3. Yea, we know Thy love rejoices
        O'er each work of Thine,
   Thou didst ears and hands and voices
        For Thy praise combine!
   Craftsman's art and music's measure
        For Thy pleasure didst design.

4. Here, great God, to-day we offer
        Of Thine own to Thee;
   And for Thine acceptance proffer,
        All unworthily,
   Hearts and minds, and hands and voices
        In our choicest melody.

103
C. M.

1. To-day's the happiest, happiest day
        Of all the happy seven;
   It is the day on which we seem
        To be most near to heaven.

2. God gave it to the rich and poor,
   To be a day of rest;
A day of holy joy and peace,
   The day we love the best.

3. On Easter Day our Lord arose
   From where He buried lay;
And every Sunday is to us
   A little Easter Day.

4. And that is why we love it so,
   And why we ever sing
Glad hymns of praise and thankful joy
   To Jesus Christ, our King.

HYMNS OF FAITH AND HOPE.

104   11s, 8s, 12s, 9s.

1. I think, when I read that sweet story of old,
   When Jesus was here among men,
How He call'd little children as lambs to His
     fold;
   I should like to have been with them then.

2. I wish that His hands had been placed on
     my head,
   That His arms had been thrown around me,
And that I might have seen His kind look
     when He said,
   "Let the little ones come unto Me."

3. Yet still to His foot-stool in pray'r I may go,
   And ask for a share in His love;
And if I thus earnestly seek Him below,
   I shall see Him and hear Him above,

4. In that beautiful place He is gone to prepare
   For all who are wash'd and forgiven;

And many dear children are gathering there,
"For of such is the kingdom of heaven."

5. I long for the joys of that glorious time,
The sweetest, and brightest, and best,
When the dear little children of every clime
Shall crowd to His arms and be blessed.

105*

1. Jesus loves the little children,
For He said one day,
"Let the children come to me,
Keep them not away."

2. There are many little children
Who have never heard
Of His love and tenderness,
Of His holy word.

3. I would tell these little children,
If they all could hear,
How he spoke to His disciples
With the children near.

4. Listen, now, while we repeat it,
Hark! 'tis very sweet;
I should think 'twould make the children
Hasten Him to meet.†

106

1. Come to Jesus, little one,
Come to Jesus now:
Humbly at His gracious throne,
In submission bow.

CHORUS.

At His feet confess your sin;
Seek forgiveness there;
For His blood can make you clean,
He will hear your prayer.

2. Seek His face without delay;
   Give Him now your heart;
Tarry not, but while you may,
   Choose the better part.—CHO.

107 H. M.

1. When little Samuel woke
     And heard his Maker's voice,
   At every word He spoke,
     How much did he rejoice!
   Oh, blessed, happy child, to find
   The God of heaven so near and kind.

2. If God would speak to me,
     And say He was my friend,
   How happy should I be!
     Oh, how would I attend!
   The smallest sin I then should fear,
   If God Almighty were so near.

3. And does he never speak?
     Oh, yes! for in His Word
   He bids me come and seek
     The God whom Samuel heard:
   In almost every page I see,
   The God of Samuel calls to me.

4. And I beneath His care
     May safely rest my head;
   I know that God is there,
     To guard my humble bed;
   And every sin I well may fear,
   Since God Almighty is so near.

108 6s, 8s.

1. Hushed was the evening hymn,
     The temple courts were dark;
   The lamp was burning dim,
     Before the sacred Ark;
   When suddenly a voice Divine
   Rang through the silence at the shrine.

2. The old man meek and mild,
   The priest of Israel, slept;
His watch the temple-child,
   The little Levite kept;
And what from Eli's sense was seal'd,
The Lord to Hannah's son revealed.

3. O! give me Samuel's ear,
   The open ear, oh, Lord,
Alive and quick to hear
   Each whisper of Thy Word;
Like him, to answer at Thy call,
And to obey Thee, first of all.

4. O! give me Samuel's heart,
   A lowly heart that waits
Where in Thy house Thou art,
   Or watches at Thy gates,
By day and night; a heart that still
Moves at the breathing of Thy will.

5. O! give me Samuel's mind,
   A sweet unmurm'ring faith,
Obedient and resign'd
   To Thee in life and death;
That I may reach, with child-like eyes,
Truths that are hidden from the wise.

109   7s.

1. Little travelers Zionward,
   Each one entering into rest,
In the kingdom of your Lord,
   In the mansions of the blest:
There to welcome Jesus waits,
   Gives the crowns His followers win:
Lift your heads, ye golden gates,
   Let the little travelers in.

2. Who are those whose little feet,
   Pacing life's dark journey through,
Now have reach'd that heavenly seat
   They had ever kept in view?

"I, from Greenland's frozen land;"
"I, from India's sultry plain:"
"I, from Africa's barren sand:"
"I, from islands of the main."

3. "All our earthly journey past,
Every tear and pain gone by,
Here together met at last
At the portal of the sky!"
Each the welcome "Come" awaits,
Conquerors over death and sin:
Lift your heads, ye golden gates,
Let the little travelers in.

110   6s, 4s, 7s.

1. There is a happy land,
Far, far away,
Where saints in glory stand,
Bright, bright as day.
Oh, how they sweetly sing,
Worthy is the Saviour King,
Loud let His praises ring,
Praise, praise for aye!

2. Come to that happy land,
Come, come away:
Why will ye doubting stand,
Why still delay?
Oh, we shall happy be,
When, from sin and sorrow free,
Lord, we shall live with Thee,
Blest, blest for aye.

3. Bright, in that happy land,
Beams every eye;
Kept by a Father's hand,
Love cannot die.
Oh, then, to glory run,
Be a crown and kingdom won,
And, bright above the sun,
We reign for aye.

111   C. M.

1. There is a green hill far away,
   Without a city wall,
   Where the dear Lord was crucified,
   Who died to save us all.

2. We may not know, we cannot tell
   What pains He had to bear,
   But we believe it was for us
   He hung and suffered there.

3. He died that we might be forgiven,
   He died to make us good,
   That we might go at last to heaven,
   Saved by His precious blood.

4. There was no other good enough
   To pay the price of sin;
   He only could unlock the gate
   Of heaven, and let us in.

5. O dearly, dearly, has He loved,
   And we must love Him, too,
   And trust in His redeeming blood,
   And try His works to do.

MISSIONS.

112*   7s.

1. When the loving Saviour
   Came a child to earth,
   Angels told the story
   Of the heavenly birth;
   How for all the children,
   On that Christmas morn,
   In the lowly manger,
   Christ, the Lord, was born.

CHORUS.
Jesus came to save us,
   Came to make us free;

---

* Written by Emma Allen.

Help to send the tidings
Over land and sea.

2. Now the dear Lord Jesus
   Back to Heaven has gone,
   But He left a message
   For us every one:
   "Go and tell the nations
   Of My wondrous love;
   How I died to bring them
   To the home above."—CHO.

3. Many little children
   For whom Jesus came,
   Do not know the Saviour,
   Never hear His Name;
   Many are in darkness,
   And, in heathen lands,
   Bow the knee to idols,
   Made with human hands.—CHO.

4. Not to holy angels
   Is such honor given.
   We can tell the lost ones
   Of the home in Heaven;
   Tell them how the Saviour
   Has for sinners died.
   Oh! the wondrous story—
   Send it far and wide.

113*

8s, 6s.

1. Hark! the merry bells are ringing,
   Children's happy voices singing,
   Joyful news to us they're bringing,
   News from far across the sea.

CHORUS.

Telling how the love of Jesus,
   Now in heathen homes is found,
Ringing out the Gospel story,
   Telling it the earth around.

* Written by Emma Allen.

2. "Boys and girls," the bells are saying,
 "Do your work without delaying;
  Many more, in darkness straying,
  Must about the Christ be told."—CHO,

3. He who died to save the children,
    He who is the children's King,
  Says that all can be His helpers,
    Other lives to Him can bring.—CHO.

4. If to serve Him, you are trying,
   Help to save the heathen dying:
   Hear how sadly they are crying,
 "Tell us of the Saviour's love."—CHO.

5. Send your gifts across the waters,
    Never mind tho' poor and small;
   If in Jesus' name they're given,
    He will take and bless them all.—CHO.

114*   8s, 7s.

1. When of old, to Zion's Temple,
    Jesus rode 'mid waving palms,
  Children's voices sang His praises,
    Hailed Him King with joyful psalms.

2. Seated on His throne in glory,
    He is still the children's Friend;
  And He bids them tell the story,
    Till to Him all nations bend.

3. They may be the chosen vessels
    Oft to bear the Gospel light;
  They may be the fairest jewels,
    Meet for Jesus' crown, so bright.

115   8s, 7s.

1. Blessed Saviour, Thou didst suffer
    Little ones to come to Thee.
  Lo! we offer now our tribute,
    Let our praise accepted be;

* Written by Catherine Dentzer.

'Mid the hallelujahs ringing,
'Mid the burst of angel song,
Stoop to hear our childish singing,
Listen to an infant throng.

2. For a cry of deepest sorrow
Comes across the waters blue:
"Ye who know salvation's story,
Haste to help and save us, too;
Shed, oh, shed the Gospel glory
O'er the darkness of our night,
Till the gloomy shadows vanish
In its full and blessed light."

3. For the poor benighted millions
We can give and work and pray,
And our gifts and prayers united,
Sure will speed that happy day,
When, no more to idols bowing,
All shall own our Jesus King,
And ten thousand voices ringing
Shall His praise victorious sing.

116 9s, 10s.

1. Pity the children across the sea,
Who never the name of Christ have heard,
Who idols worship on bended knee,
Which see not and hear not a single word.

2. Pity the children across the sea.
The Master proclaims in a voice of love,
"Suffer the children to come to Me,
Of such is the kingdom of God above."

117* 7s.

1. Once again. dear Lord, we pray
For the children far away,
Who have never even heard
Jesus' name, that sweetest word.

* From Missionary Hymnal, by permission.

2. Little lips that Thou hast made,
   Murm'ring in the temple's shade,
   Give to gods of wood and stone,
   Praise that should be all Thine own.

3. Little hands, whose wondrous skill
   Thou hast giv'n to do Thy will.
   Off'rings bring and serve with fear
   Gods that cannot see or hear.

4. Teach them, O, Thou heav'nly King,
   All their gifts and praise to bring,
   To Thy Son, who died to prove
   Thy forgiving, saving love.

WORK.

118   6s, 4s.

1. Onward, Christian soldiers,
      Marching as to war,
   With the cross of Jesus
      Going on before.
   Christ, the royal Master,
      Leads against the foe;
   Forward into battle
      See His banners go.

CHORUS.

   Onward, Christian soldiers,
      Marching as to war,
   With the cross of Jesus
      Going on before.

2. Like a mighty army,
      Moves the Church of God;
   Brothers, we are treading
      Where the saints have trod;
   We are not divided,

All one body we,
One in hope and doctrine,
One in charity.—CHO.

3. Crowns and thrones may perish,
   Kingdoms rise and wane,
But the Church of Jesus
   Constant will remain.
Gates of hell can never
   'Gainst that Church prevail;
We have Christ's own promise,
   And that cannot fail.—CHO.

4. Onward, then, ye people,
   Join our happy throng;
Blend with ours your voices
   In the triumph song;
Glory, laud, and honor
   Unto Christ the King:
This thro' countless ages
   Men and angels sing.—CHO.

119

1. Forward! be our watchword,
   Steps and voices joined;
Seek the things before us,
   Not a look behind:
Burns the fiery pillar
   At our army's head;
Who shall dream of shrinking,
   By our Captain led?
Forward through the desert,
   Through the toil and fight:
Jordan flows before us,
   Zion beams with light.

2. Forward, when in childhood
   Buds the infant mind;
All through youth and manhood,
   Not a thought behind:
Speed through realms of nature,

Climb the steps of grace;
　Faint not, till in glory
　　Gleams our Father's face.
Forward, all the lifetime,
　Climb from height to height:
Till the head be hoary,
　Till the eve be light.

3. Glories upon glories
　　Hath our God prepared,
　By the souls that love Him
　　One day to be shared;
Eye hath not beheld them,
　Ear hath never heard;
Nor of these hath uttered
　Thought or speech a word:
Forward, marching eastward,
　Where the heaven is bright,
Till the veil be lifted,
　Till our faith be sight!

120*

1. I'm a little pilgrim,
　And I'll march along,
Doing what I can for Jesus;
　For He loves me dearly,
　And He'll make me strong,
If I put my trust in Him.
CHORUS.
I'm a little pilgrim, yes, yes, yes!
　Come and see, come and see
How the heavenly Father loves to bless
　Little children just like me!

2. I'm a little pilgrim,
　Working for the right,
Doing little deeds for Jesus:

* By permission of David C. Cook Pub. Co.

Won't you come and help me,
  Walking in the light?
Come and put your trust in Him.—CHO.

3. I'm a little pilgrim,
    Telling ev'ry one
All about the love of Jesus;
When my journey's ended,
    And my work is done,
Christ will take me home to Him.—CHO.

121

7s.

1. Little builders all are we,
Builders for eternity;
Children of the Mission Bands,
Working with our hearts and hands
Building temples for our King,
By the offerings we bring;
Living temples He doth raise,
Fill'd with life and light and praise.

2. One by one the stones we lay,
Building slowly, day by day;
Building for our love are we,
In the lands beyond the sea;
Building by each thought and pray'r,
For the souls that suffer there;
Building in the Hindoo land,
Where the idols are as sand.

3. On mount Lebanon's fair heights,
By our many gathered mites,
Where the Nile's sweet waters pour;
Building all the wide world o'er:
And one day our eyes shall see,
In a glad eternity,
"Living stones" we helped to bring
For the palace of our King.

122* 12s, 9s.

1. There is something on earth for the children
    to do,
  Ere they go to the beautiful land;
  There's a pathway of love where the young-
    est may go,
  And employment for each little hand.

CHORUS.

There is something to do, there is something
    to do,
  There is something for children to do;
To lead others to love the dear Saviour above,
  There is something for children to do.

2. Tho' it may be but little, our Saviour once
    said,
  If the little be given in love,
  To the thirsty a drink, to the hungry some
    bread,
  'Twill be surely rewarded above.—CHO.

3. And the children can tell the sweet story
    of old,
  Tell of Him by whom sin is forgiv'n;
  And the angels of God will rejoice if one
    soul
  Should be led by the children to heaven.
                                    —CHO.

123 7s, 6s, 8s, 6s.

1. Oh, what can little hands, little hands do
    To please the King of heaven?
  The little hands some work may try
  To help the poor in misery—
    Such grace to mine be given.

---

* By permission of David C. Cook Pub. Co.

2. Oh, what can little lips, little lips do
    To please the King of heaven?
  The little lips can praise and pray,
  And gentle words of kindness say—
    Such grace to mine be given.

3. Oh, what can little eyes, little eyes do
    To please the King of heaven?
  The little eyes can upward look,
  Can learn to read God's holy book—
    Such grace to mine be given.

4. Oh, what can little hearts, little hearts do
    To please the King of heaven?
  The hearts, if God His Spirit send,
  Can love and trust the children's Friend—
    Such grace to mine be given.

5. When hearts and hands and lips unite
    To please the King of heaven,
  And serve the Saviour with delight,
  They are most precious in His sight—
    Such grace to mine be given.

124   8s, 6s.

1. I cannot do great things for Him
    Who did so much for me,
  But I should like to show my love,
    Dear Jesus, unto Thee;
  Faithful in very little things,
    O Saviour, may I be.

2. There are small things, in daily life,
    In which I may obey,
  And thus may show my love to Thee;
    And always, ev'ry day,
  There are some little loving words
    Which I for Thee may say.

3. There are small crosses I may take,
    Small burdens I may bear,

Small acts of faith and deeds of love,
  Some sorrows I may share;
And little bits of work for Thee
  I may do ev'rywhere.

4. So I ask Thee to give me grace,
  My little place to fill,
That I may ever walk with Thee,
  And ever do Thy will;
That in each duty, great or small,
  I may be faithful still.

125
7s, 6s.

1. What can I give to Jesus,
  Who gave His life for me?
How can I show my love to Him
  Who died on Calvary?
I'll give my heart to Jesus,
  In childhood's tender spring,
I know that He will not despise
  The offering that I bring.

2. I'll give my soul to Jesus,
  And calmly, gladly rest
Its youthful hopes and fond desires
  Upon His loving breast.
I'll give my mind to Jesus,
  And seek in thoughtful hours
His Spirit's grace, to consecrate
  Its early opening powers.

3. I'll give my strength to Jesus
  Of foot, of head, of will;
Run where He sends, and ever strive
  His pleasure to fulfill.
I'll give my time to Jesus;
  Oh, that each hour might be
Filled up with holy work for Him,
  Who spent His life for me.

126*

7s, 5s.

1. We are little gleaners brave,
     Toiling all the day,
   In the vineyard of the Lord,
     Bearing sheaves away;
   Faithful gleaners will we prove,
     Trusting in our Saviour's love;
   We are little gleaners brave,
     Gleaning for the Lord.

CHORUS.

Little gleaners for the Lord,
  Happy we, happy we,
Gleaning in the field so broad,
  Gleaning for the Lord.

2. We are little gleaners brave,
     In the vineyard wide;
   There is work for all to do,
     There will we abide;
   Tares are scattered ev'rywhere,
     We must search them out with care;
   We are little gleaners brave,
     Gleaning for the Lord.—CHO.

? We are little gleaners brave,
     Harvest time goes by;
   Come and help. there's room for all,
     Stand not idly by:
   All the faithful, valiant band
   Christ will crown in glory-land;
     We are little gleaners brave,
   Gleaning for the Lord.—CHO.

127

8s, 6s.

1. We are a little gleaning band,
     We cannot bind the sheaves,
   But we can follow Him who reaps,
     And gather what He leaves;

---

* By permission of David C. Cook Pub. Co.

We are not strong, but Jesus loves
  The weakest of the fold,
And in our feeble efforts proves
  His tenderness, untold.

2. We are not rich, but we can give,
  As we are passing on,
A cup of water, in His name,
  To some poor fainting one;
We are not wise, but Christ, our Lord,
  Revealed to babes His will,
And we are sure, from His dear word,
  He saves the children still.

3. We know that with our gathered grain
  Briars and leaves are seen;
Yet, since we tried, He smiles the same,
  And takes our offering.
Dear children, still Hosanna sing,
  As Christ doth conquering come,
Cast in your treasures as He brings
  The heathen nations home.

128   8s, 7s, 4s.

1. In the vineyard of our Father,
  Daily work we find to do;
Scattered gleanings we may gather,
  Though we are but young and few;
      Little clusters
  Help to fill the garners, too.

2. Toiling early in the morning,
  Catching moments thro' the day,
Nothing small or lowly scorning,
  So along our path we stray;
      Gathering gladly
  Free-will offerings by the way.

3. Not for selfish praise or glory,
  Not for objects nothing worth,
But to send the blessed story

Of the Gospel o'er the earth,
Telling mortals
Of our Lord and Saviour's birth.

4 Steadfast, then, in our endeavor,
Heavenly Father, may we be;
And, for ever and for ever,
We will give the praise to Thee;
Hallelujah!
Singing all eternally.

129   7s.

1. Little givers, come and bring
Tribute to your heav'nly King;
Lay it on the altar high,
While your songs ascend the sky.

2. Little givers, do your part,
With a glad and willing heart;
For the angel voices say,
Little givers, give to-day.

3. Give to all the darkened earth
Tidings of a heav'nly birth;
Till the youth in ev'ry land
Learn the Saviour's sweet command.

130*   11s.

1. Dear Jesus, we bring Thee our off'rings
to-day;
We give Thee our voices—accept them,
we pray;
Our hands for Thy service, our feet for
Thy ways,
Our hearts for Thy dwelling, our lips for
Thy praise.
We bring gifts to Jesus,
We bring gifts to-day—
Our all give Thee, Jesus—
Accept us, we pray.

---

* By permission of David C. Cook Pub. Co.

2. Our eyes to behold Thee in earth, sea
and sky,
And see Thee again in the poor passer-by;
Our hands to bring off'rings, and gifts
for the poor,
Our hearts to swing open to Jesus the door.
We bring gifts, etc.

3. Our minds, too, to study Thy glorious
Word,
Our hearing to list to Thy voice, precious
Lord;
Our bodies, Thy temple, our souls for Thy
throne.
We bring Thee ourselves, Lord, to be all
Thine own.
We bring gifts, etc.

131

1. 'Twas only a drop in the bucket,
But each little drop will tell;
The bucket would soon be empty
Without the drops in the well.
'Twas only a poor little penny—
It was all I had to give;
But as pennies make the dollars,
It may help some cause to live.

CHORUS.

God loveth the cheerful giver,
Though the gift be ever so small;
But what doth He think of His children
If they never give at all?

2. 'Twas only some out-grown garments,
'Twas all that I had to spare,
But they will help clothe the needy—
The poor are everywhere;
A word, now and then, of comfort,
That cost me naught to say,
But they cheered the weary pilgrim,
And helped him on his way.—CHO.

Closing Hymns and Doxologies.

132 7s, 6s.

1. The whole wide world for Jesus!
   Once more before we part,
   Ring out the joyful watchword
   From every grateful heart.
   The whole wide world for Jesus!
   Be this our battle-cry;
   The Crucified shall conquer,
   The victory is nigh.

2. The whole wide world for Jesus!
   From out the Golden Gate,
   Through all the South Sea Islands,
   To China's princely state;
   From India's vales and mountains,
   Through Persia's land of bloom,
   To storied Palestina
   And Africa's desert gloom.

3. The whole wide world for Jesus!
   Its hearts and homes and thrones;
   Ring out again the watchword
   In loud and joyous tones.
   The whole wide world for Jesus!
   With prayer the song we'll sing,
   And speed the prayer with labor,
   Till earth shall crown Him King.

133 7s.

1. For a season called to part,
   Let us now ourselves commend
   To the gracious eye and heart
   Of our ever-present Friend.

2. Jesus, hear our humble prayer!
   Tender Shepherd of Thy sheep,

Let Thy mercy and Thy care.
All our souls in safety keep.

3. In Thy strength may we be strong,
Sweeten every cross and pain;
Give us, if we live, ere long
In Thy peace to meet again.

4. Then, if Thou Thy help afford,
Ebenezers shall be reared;
And our souls shall praise the Lord.
Who our poor petitions heard.

134   10s.

1. Abide with me; fast falls the even-tide;
The darkness deepens: Lord, with me abide!
When other helpers fail, and comforts flee,
Help of the helpless, oh, abide with me!

2. Not a brief glance I beg, a passing word,
But as Thou dwell'st with Thy disciples, Lord,
Familiar, condescending, patient, free,
Come, not to sojourn, but abide with me.

3. I need Thy presence every passing hour;
What but Thy grace can foil the tempter's
power?
Who like Thyself my guide and stay can be?
Through cloud and sunshine, oh, abide with
me.

4. Hold Thou Thy Cross before my closing eyes,
Shine through the gloom, and point me to
the skies:
Heaven's morning breaks, and earth's vain
shadows flee;
In life, in death, O Lord, abide with me!

135   L. M.

1. Sun of my soul, Thou Saviour dear,
It is not night if Thou be near;
Oh, may no earth-born cloud arise,
To hide Thee from Thy servant's eyes.

2. When soft the dews of kindly sleep
My wearied eyelids gently steep,
Be my last thought—how sweet to rest
Forever on my Saviour's breast.

3. Abide with me from morn till eve,
For without Thee I cannot live;
Abide with me when night is nigh,
For without Thee I dare not die.

4. Be near to bless me when I wake,
Ere through the world my way I take;
Abide with me till, in Thy love,
I lose myself in heaven above.

136   8, 7s, 4s.

1. God of our salvation, hear us;
Bless, oh, bless us, e'er we go!
When we join the world, be near us,
Lest we cold and careless grow;
Saviour, keep us—
Keep us safe from every foe.

2. As our steps are drawing nearer
To our best and lasting home,
May our view of heaven grow clearer,
Hope more bright of joys to come;
And when dying,
May Thy presence cheer the gloom.

137   H. M.

1. Dear Father, ere we part,
Now let Thy grace descend,
And fill each youthful heart
With peace from Christ, our Friend;
May showers of blessings from above
Descend and fill our hearts with love.

2. May we, in after years,
With gratitude review
The service of this day,

The work we now pursue,
And speed our way to worlds above,
With hearts all fired with holy love.

138   6s, 5s.

1. Now the day is over,
     Night is drawing nigh,
   Shadows of the evening
     Steal across the sky.

2. Now the darkness gathers,
     Stars begin to peep,
   Birds, and beasts. and flowers
     Soon will be asleep.

3. Jesus, give the weary
     Calm and sweet repose,
   With Thy tenderest blessing
     May my eyelids close.

4. Through the long night-watches
     May Thine angels spread
   Their white wings above me,
     Watching round my bed.

5. When the morning wakens,
     Then may I arise,
   Pure, and fresh. and sinless
     In Thy Holy Eyes.

139   S. M.

1. Blest be the tie that binds
     Our hearts in Christian love;
   The fellowship of kindred minds
     Is like to that above.

2. Before our Father's throne
     We pour our ardent prayers;
   Our fears, our hopes, our aims are one,
     Our comforts and our cares.

3. We share our mutual woes,
     Our mutual burdens bear;

And often for each other flows
The sympathizing tear.

4. When we asunder part,
   It gives us inward pain;
   But we shall still be joined in heart,
   And hope to meet again.

5. From sorrow, toil, and pain,
   And sin, we shall be free;
   And perfect love and friendship reign
   Through all eternity.

140   7s.

1. Now may He, who from the dead,
   Brought the Shepherd of the sheep,
   Jesus Christ, our King and Head,
   All our souls in safety keep!

2. May He teach us to fulfill
   What is pleasing in His sight;
   Perfect us in all His will,
   And preserve us day and night!

· 3. Great Redeemer! Thee we praise,
   Who the covenant sealed with blood;
   While our hearts and voices raise
   Loud thanksgivings unto God.

141   P. M.

1. If 'tis sweet to mingle where
   Christians meet for social prayer;
   If 'tis sweet with them to raise
   Songs of holy joy and praise—
   Passing sweet that state must be
   Where they meet eternally.

2. Saviour, may these meetings prove
   Preparations for above;
   While we worship in this place,
   May we grow from grace to grace,
   Till we, each, in his degree,
   Fit for endless glory be.

142 S. M.

1. Lord, at this closing hour,
   Establish every heart
Upon Thy word of truth and power,
   To keep us when we part.

2. Peace to our brethren give;
   Fill all our hearts with love;
In faith and patience may we live,
   And seek our rest above.

3. Through changes, bright or drear,
   We would Thy will pursue;
And toil to spread Thy kingdom here,
   Till we its glory view.

4. To God, the only wise,
   In every age adored,
Let glory from the Church arise,
   Through Jesus Christ, our Lord!

143 S. M

1. Once more, before we part,
   Great God, attend our prayer,
And seal the Gospel on the heart
   Of all assembled here.

2. And if we meet no more
   On Zion's holy ground,
Oh, may we reach that blissful shore
   Whither Thy saints are bound.

144 8s, 7s, 4s.

1. Lord, dismiss us with Thy blessing—
   Fill our hearts with joy and peace;
Let us each, Thy love possessing,
   Triumph in redeeming grace;
      Oh, refresh us!
Traveling through this wilderness.

2. Thanks we give, and adoration,
   For Thy Gospel's joyful sound;

May the fruits of Thy salvation
In our hearts and lives abound;
May Thy presence
With us evermore be found.

3. So, whene'er the signal's given,
Us from earth to call away,
Borne on angel's wings to heaven,
Glad to leave our cumbrous clay,
May we, ready,
Rise and reign in endless day!

145 L. M.

1. Dismiss us with Thy blessing, Lord;
Help us to feed upon Thy word;
All that has been amiss, forgive,
And let Thy truth within us live.

2. Though we are guilty, Thou art good:
Wash all our works in Jesus' blood;
Give every fettered soul release,
And bid us all depart in peace.

146*

1. God be with you till we meet again,
By His counsels guide, uphold you,
With His sheep securely fold you.
God be with you till we meet again.

CHORUS.
Till we meet, till we meet,
Till we meet at Jesus' feet;
Till we meet, till we meet,
God be with you till we meet again.

2. God be with you till we meet again,
'Neath His wings securely hide you,
Daily manna still divide you,
God be with you till we meet again.—CHO.

---

* By permission of Rev. J. E. Rankin, D. D., Washington, D. C.

3. God be with you till we meet again;
   When life's perils thick confound you,
   Put His arms unfailing round you:
God be with you till we meet again.—CHO.

4. God be with you till we meet again,
   Keep love's banner floating o'er you,
   Smite death's threat'ning wave before
      you;
God be with you till we meet again.—CHO.

147   8s.

1. May the grace of Christ, our Saviour,
   And the Father's boundless love,
With the Holy Spirit's favor,
   Rest upon us from above.
Thus may we abide in union
   With each other and the Lord,
And possess, in sweet communion,
   Joys which earth cannot afford.

148   L. M.

1. To God the Father, God the Son,
   And God the Spirit, Three in One,
   Be honor, praise, and glory given,
   By all on earth and all in heaven.

149   L. M.

1. Praise God, from whom all blessings flow,
   Praise Him, all creatures here below:
   Praise Him above, ye heavenly host,
   Praise Father, Son, and Holy Ghost.

150   S. M.

1. Ye angels round the throne,
   And saints that dwell below,
Worship the Father, praise the Son,
   And bless the Spirit, too.

151 C. M.

1. Now let the Father, and the Son,
    And Spirit be adored,
Where there are works to make Him known,
    Or saints to love the Lord.

152 7s.

1. Sing we to our God above,
    Praise eternal as His love;
    Praise Him, all ye heavenly host,
    Father, Son, and Holy Ghost.

153 8s, 7s, 4s.

1. Great Jehovah! we adore Thee,
    God the Father—God the Son—
God the Spirit—joined in glory,
    On the same eternal throne;
        Endless praises
    To Jehovah, Three in One.

154 6s, 4s.

1. To God—the Father, Son,
    And Spirit—Three in One,
        All praise be given!
    Crown Him in ev'ry song;
    To Him your hearts belong;
    Let all His praise prolong,
        On earth, in heaven.

INDEX.

ORDER OF SERVICE.

INDEX OF HYMNS.

178

INDEX OF TUNES.

* Published by Woman's Board of Missions, 53 Dearborn Street, Chicago, Ill.

* Repeat first two syllables of last line.

113.*
114. Talmer. Book of Worship, . . 108.
115. Ripley.   "   "   "   . . 154.
116. Missionary Hymnal, ... 16.
117.   "   "   . . . . 31.
118. Augsburg Songs, No. 1, . . . 178.
119.   "   "   "   . . . "
120.† Primary Songs,   . . . 27.
121. Litany. Book of Worship. . . 237.
122. Primary Songs, ... 57.
123. Happy Voices, ... 136.
124. Missionary Hymnal, ... 34.
125.   "   "   . . . . . "
126. Primary Songs, ... 9.
127. Missionary Hymnal, ... 40.
128. Alvan. Book of Worship, . . 27.
129. Missionary Hymnal, ... 6.
130. Primary Songs, ... 24.
131.‡
132. Mendebras. Book of Worship, . 41.
133. Eshtemva.   "   "   "   . 437.
134. Eventide.   "   "   "   . 532.
135. Hursley,   "   "   "   • . 530.
136. Alvan.   "   "   "   . 27.
137. Lischer.   "   "   "   . 35.
138. Sunday School Book, (Gen. Council.) 51.
139. Dennis. Book of Worship, . . 434.
140. Solitude.   "   "   "   . . 599.

---

* Will appear in our proposed Missionary Hymnal.
† David C. Cook Pub. Co., Chicago, Ill.
‡ Will appear in our proposed Missionary Hymnal.

141.	Rosefield.	Book of Worship.	.	317.
142.	Addison.	" " "	. .	32.
143.	Olmutz.	" " "	. .	596.
144.	Zion.	" " "	. .	278.
145.	Ward.	" " "	. .	80.
146.	Gospel Hymns, No. 6, (C. E. ed.)		.	209.
147.	Bavaria.	Book of Worship,	. .	150.
148.	Old Hundred.	" " "	. .	1.
149.	" "	" " "	. .	1.
150.	Boylston.	" " "	. .	308.
152.	Downs.	" " "	. .	354.
152	Horton.	" " "	. .	276.
153.	Zion.	" " "	. .	278.
154.	Italian Hymn.	" " "	. .	66.